The Betrayal of Ethiopia

by Assefa Adefris

[illegible]

1998 USA

Photo acknowledgments:
The following libraries have graciously provided pictures included in this book: The Library of Congress, Washington, DC; The United States National Archives, College Park, Maryland; The Truman Library, Independence, Kansas; The Eisenhower Library, Abilene, Kansas, and The John F. Kennedy Library, Boston, Massachusetts. The following individuals have also provided pictures for this book: Lynda Johnson Robb and Senator Charles Robb; Dr. Johnson of Loma Linda, California, former director of the Empress Zaudita Hospital, Addis Ababa, Ethiopia; Mr. Tony Boydjian; Ato Tesfaye, former photographer of the Ministry of Information of Ethiopia, assigned as His Majesty's special photographer.

Printed in the United States of America

Published by The American Ethiopian Press
6901 Ben Franklin Rd.
Springfield, VA 22150
703 451-8308

Book and cover design by Griffith Publishing Consultants
Caldwell, Idaho

ISBN 0-9659079-0-2

Table of Contents

Acknowledgments

First and foremost I would like to thank my lovely wife, Amsale Hailu, for standing by me and being supportive through all of our ups and downs, for which we hold responsible the communist cadres of Mengistu Hailemariam, Ethiopia. Although we suffered a 95° downward change in our lives, my wife and children interpreted this simply as a misfortune that befell us and accepted it gracefully, as a spiritual challenge to our family.

To our children—Ted, Mekdelawit, Adefris and young Ezana Adefris: My thanks for making us proud parents. The difficult life transition did not distract them from pursuing their educational convictions. Ted and Mekdealwit graduated with honors from their respective universities, and Adefris has graduated from UVA.

All of the following people have touched our lives in very personal ways. I want to express my deep gratitude to each of them for their generosity and giving spirit. My family and I will always remember them:

Curt and Barbara Taylor of Sacramento, California, who made my initiation to the United States infinitely smoother by affording my family much needed help. They rented a home for us, provided basic needs for more than a year, and took us job searching time after time.

Former Board of Supervisors of Santa Clara, current U.S. Congresswoman Zoe Lofgren of San Jose, California, who helped bring the community together and assisted us with fund-raising for the community organization.

Former US Congressman Norman Mineta, San Jose, California.

David Nielson, of Mountain View, California, who was always there to help us with financial and other needs.

David Marion of San Jose, California, who provided me with any legal advice I needed.

Kebede Gashaw, of Sacramento, California, and a high school friend. He and his wife gave generous help to me and my family.

C. O. Davis of San Jose, California, who was there for us in the trying days after our arrival in California.

Carol Beddo, former San Jose Mayor's Assistant. She was instrumental in the success of my community organization in San Jose.

Former State Senator John Garamendi of Stockton, California, who was the most helpful of all to our start-up organization and our ultimate success in California. John is currently United States Deputy Secretary of the Interior.

John and Alicia Gaddis, who offered their good friendship to our three children.

Paul Christenson of Sunnyvale, California, who provided office equipment and financial support during my stay in California.

Yilma Gulteneh, Professor at Howard University, Washington DC, and my friend of 33 years, whom I could always count on for being there when it mattered.

Louis Kramp of Oakton, Virginia, whose ongoing moral support and advice I value highly.

Colonel Maru Gatew of Ethiopia, a dear friend who taught me more about Ethiopian history than any university professor. His fatherly advice and encouragement made me a stronger and better person.

Albert W. Blackburn of McLean, Virginia, for his assistance and advice.

Georg Marge Lis of Springfield, Virtinia.

Joyce Griffith of Idaho, for her patience and cooperation.

Last, but not least, Elizabeth Bourke, of Oakton, Virginia, formerly of Ireland. She helped with writing projects and advice, and continues to provide support when I need it.

Thank You, America!

When the communist revolution began in Ethiopia in 1974, my wife Amsale and I were happy, prosperous business people with a four-year-old son, Theodrose. By 1976 there were two additions to the family, Mekdalawit and Adefris Jr. Unfortunately, peace and stability were destroyed by the political powers that seized control of Ethiopia, and I was imprisoned. If not for our great fortune in escaping Ethiopia, I would be a dead man now. We found our way to England for a few years and then moved on to the United States where we have lived since then.

I am grateful to America for many reasons. First, because I was able to save my family and myself from the communists and, in turn, provide my children with the best education America has to offer. My oldest son, Ted, graduated from the University of California at Davis. My daughter Mikie graduated from Old Dominion University. My son Ady graduated with distinction from the University of Virginia. My American-born son, Izana, is attending the Garfield Elementary School in northern Virginia.

The second reason I am grateful to America is that the laws of this country permit me to express myself freely without fear or restriction. For these and many other reasons I am thankful that I was able to find peace and freedom for my family in America.

—Assefa Adefris

Author's Note

My intention in writing this book is not to portray Emperor Haile Selassie as a perfect person. Like all human beings, he certainly had negative as well as positive attributes. My intention, rather, is to bring forth historical facts that have been ignored throughout the years. Many defamatory statements have been written about the Emperor by those with leftist political views and by those with vested political interests in weakening and exploiting Ethiopia. This view is evidenced by the links of some European writers with the effort to break Eritrea away from the rest of Ethiopia. There seems to be a cozy relationship between EPLF leaders and many of these writers.

These writers gave slanted interpretations of history in order to diminish the Emperor's standing and thereby Ethiopia's stature in the eyes of Ethiopia's youth who have been schooled in a "modern" (Western) school system. It has become painfully evident to many young Ethiopians that they have been seductively misled into working for the disintegration of their own country and the mass murder of their families and friends.

Emperor Haile Selassie's personality, his speeches, and his State policies along with the love he exhibited for his country and his people stand as a tribute to his unflinching sense of pride and independence. Foreign interests and their paid writers never understood this independence. They put all their craft to work to belittle Haile Selassie in the eyes of Ethiopians and the rest of the world. The truth must be recorded so that those who would detract from Ethiopia's past will not succeed.

To Date Unburied Remains

The visionary Emperor of Ethiopia who brought his country into the modern status of Twentieth Century, has been denied burial in the country where he was born, struggled and fought for in the liberation from fascist Italy and all other historical enemies of Ethiopia from all directions.

Emperor Haile Selassie was once known as the father of modern day Africa and the child of Ethiopia because he dedicated himself to the struggle against the colonization of Africa. He united the Ethiopian people and reformed the Ethiopian society in his attempt to stamp out all traditional forms of oppression as well as forging a strong and modern Ethiopia. His tools were first providing good education for young Ethiopians; second training and establishing a strong defense army and third, in order to accomplish his plans, cooperation with the United States was vital. His relations with these three groups on which he had hoped to base his effectiveness as a reformed, i.e. educated Ethiopians, the Ethiopian defense forces and the post-war American administrations was like a love affair while it lasted.

Ironically, these very same three groups turned out to be the central actors to expedite the decline and ultimate demise of his reign and with it, the decline and the present process of disintegration of the Ethiopian state. That state was so laboriously built by the Emperor over decades alter the liberation from fascist Italy's attempt to colonize and destroy historical Ethiopia. The United States government that once supported and promoted the unification of the Italian-occupied Eritrea to its motherland, historical Ethiopia, has recently officially and actively supported and promoted the disintegration of Ethiopia and continues to do so to date. This is a source of puzzlement for learned Ethiopians as well as others, as to what rationale was used by the American policy advisors and policy shapers. At any rate, the Emperor was betrayed in his life and even in his death, as his remains have not been properly buried to this day. The present land-nationalizing communist style regime in Ethiopia, that is supported by American tax-payer money, is carrying its revenge against the person, the history and goals of the Emperor to build a united Ethiopia along the values of the Western political system.

Emperor Haile Selassie pens a letter to US President Franklin D. Roosevelt during a 1941 visit by an American delegation to Addis Ababa. The letter was rushed by Army plane to the White House.

Man of the Year

By Harold G. Marcus

Above all, Haile Selassie has created a general, warm and blind sympathy for uncivilized Ethiopia throughout civilized Christendom. In the wake of the world's grandiose Depression, with millions of white men uncertain as to the benefits of civilization, 1935 produced a peculiar Spirit of the Year in which it was felt to be a crying shame that the Machine Age seemed about to intrude upon Africa's last free, unscathed and simple people. They were *ipso facto* Noble Savages, and the noblest Ethiopian of them all naturally emerged as Man of the Year... Outside Italy, the Emperor was clapped and cheered during 1935 in almost every cinema house in the world. His name entered the U.S. vocabulary in such homely exclamations as, "Well! If that's so, then I'm Haile Selassie!"...Without quibble or qualification the best and wisest ruler ancient Ethiopia has ever had is the present Man of the Year.

—January 6, 1936, *Time Mgazine*

1

HAILE SELASSIE: PORTRAIT OF A LEADER

Emperor Haile Selassie I was probably the most universally respected and revered national leader ever produced by the African continent.

Unfortunately, he is a receding memory in the American consciousness today. I was jolted into recognition of this unfortunate fact by a visit to the White House, where I took my son, who was six years old, on a visitors' tour. At one point of the tour the walls are lined with pictures of heads of states who have been guests of the American government through the years. In the judgment of history, many of these leaders are unimportant—and I do not mean to denigrate them as leaders of their people—but why was the photographic display not graced by one of the most important national figures of our time, Haile Selassie I?

It could not be for lack of available pictures. The fact that I, as a private citizen, have access to numerous news photos of the Emperor's visits to several US presidents, suggests that govern-

Ezana A. Adefris, the author's young son visited the White House with his father.

ment files are full of such pictures. The absence of a single picture on a White House wall must surely be an oversight by the staff responsible for the display. But in this instance, such an oversight may spring from a fading memory of the man. As an Ethiopian living happily in this country and as a personal witness of His Majesty Emperor Haile Selassie I, as a proud father of sons and a daughter who have graduated from American universities and another who is currently in elementary school in this country and loving it, I dedicate the following pages to all of them and to my wife, Amsale. Like me, Amsale lost most of her family and all of her property when the regime of Mengistu Haile Mariam overthrew and eventually murdered Emperor Haile Selassie—the man who created modern Ethiopia—thereby opening the way to the slaughter of the nation's most progressive leadership in politics, agriculture and industry.

When Royal Regent Negus Teferi

The emperor reading a book in the White House library during a state visit to the United States in May 1954.

became Emperor Haile Selassie I in 1930, Ethiopia had changed little since biblical times. Slavery was commonplace. Illiteracy was the norm. Subsistence agriculture was the cornerstone of existence for the entire society, and was supported by all segments of the society—peasants, priests, aristocrats. Ethiopia was not in step with the world. The Emperor, a brilliant student of world history as well as that of his own nation, had spent his youthful years envisioning what he might do to bring his country into the modern world when and if he came to power.

Much of the rest of the world—Britain, Europe, the Americas and Japan—had been transformed by the industrial revolution starting in the late eighteenth century. Agriculture had been mechanized and made vastly more productive. Slavery had long since been abolished. Education had become the birthright of the great majority of people, though higher education had not yet become available to all.

In 1930, the Ethiopian government and most of the people still regarded work performed by machines as inferior to work done by the human hand. "What could a machine do that men could not do better?" was the common view. Moreover, for nearly all of its 3,000-year history, Ethiopia was a country without private ownership of land.

Individuals could use the land for agricultural pursuits, for hunting, for building their own homes, but ownership belonged to the country for use by all the people. Though noble and egalitarian in practice and intent, this concept of land use was a deterrent to industrial development. Financing and the know-how required to build an industry would have to come primarily from foreign capitalists, who did not look kindly on common ownership of the land on which they would build. Formal education at any level within Ethiopia was still virtually unknown. Occasionally the sons of well-to-do farmers or provisional authorities were sent abroad to study, but the national view of a well-educated man was distrust and even hostility.

There was no central government. Power and public order were in the hands of provincial leaders known by titles such as Ras, Dejazmach, Garada, Koro, Tona and Tato (King of Kaffa), Balabat and several others. These local leaders were appointed by the Emperor, but thereafter ran their provinces as they wished. The idea of a senate or a parliament or any other kind of power sharing was alien to the governance of Ethiopia, provincially or nationally.

This was the state of affairs in 1930 when Haile Selassie assumed the throne after two years in the lesser position of king. His first imperial act was to ban the feudal systems that existed in the provinces and to give the nation its first constitution and parliamentary body. The real power in the parliament resided in the senate, whose members were chosen by the Emperor, but there was also a chamber of deputies dominated by provincial chieftains, which at least gave local governments a voice in national decisions.

It was the Emperor's intention that the chamber of deputies would evolve into a popularly elected branch of government that would initiate policies, rather than just rubber stamping them. He did not allow for this at the beginning because he felt that some basic national reforms would be essential to the success of a truly democratic legislative body.

Education was his top priority reform. The goal was to provide educational opportunity for all who wanted it. In all parts of the country schools had to be built and staffed. Democratic values had to be learned, appreciated and practiced wherever possible. For the next several years he spent heavily in converting older buildings into classrooms and constructing new schools from the ground up. Creating places in which teaching could take place proved far easier than finding the teachers—few Ethiopians possessed the needed skills. But thanks to the Emperor's personal efforts to recruit qualified people from other nations, a small army of teachers from abroad—mainly the United States and Great Britain—accepted teaching assignments in Addis Ababa and many provincial population centers. This would not have been possible if Haile Selassie not been so well respected around the world. The education program got off to a very good start.

His second priority reform was the abolition of slavery. He banned this ancient practice in 1930, by executive fiat, but was not surprised to find that acceptance among the power elite was slow in coming. He had little enforcement ability in the far-flung provinces, which were ruled by tradition-bound, oftentimes tyrannical officials, or rases. Success came first in Addis Ababa where he had some enforcement power, and was slowly winning observance elsewhere, when international affairs intruded on the domestic scene.

The year was 1935. The intruder was Benito Mussolini, dictator of Italy. Already an occupier of Eritrea,* he served notice on Emperor Haile Selassie that he intended to take over all of Ethiopia. Ethiopia's greatest modern crisis had begun, and all domestic reform activities were put on hold.

Mussolini carried out his threat in October 1935, invading with a huge army and capturing Addis Ababa. The Emperor was forced to flee the country, finding protection in Britain. He went immediately to the League of Nations to plead for international support, in language that elevated him to a leadership role in the world's conscience. But his words fell on deaf ears, and two years later he returned to renew the argument for collective security, this time against a background of European terrorism being carried out in Nazi Germany. Again, the League of Nations failed. After the meeting he announced to the world: "Don't they understand that they

**Eritrea is an Italian name given to the northern Ethiopian region, including the Red Sea Coast. The historic name of this region was Bahre Negash (Sea of the King).*

Table1: Students in high school or college in Ethiopia in 1972

Province	Gov't	Other	Total
Arusi	20,209	3,607	23,816
Bale	7,651	1,342	8,903
Begemider	26,597	1,711	28,308
Eritrea	60,781	34,895	95,676
Gomu Gofta	10,422	913	11,335
Gojjam	26,714	1,114	27,862
Hararge	29,854	9,145	38,999
Illubabor	17,336	281	17,617
Kafta	16,285	2,590	18,875
Shao	75,811	17,271	93,082
Addis Ababa	62,092	39,075	101,170
Sidamo	28,082	8,848	36,930
Tigre	21,660	5,855	27,515
Wollega	30,720	13,605	44,325
Wollo	25,512	2,918	28,430

Complaints are frequently heard that Eritrea, now an independent country, was administered unfairly by Ethiopia. In fact, the allocation of resources was evenhanded, as shown in the above table showing great benefits to all provinces in education. Had Haile Sellasie's record continued up to his untimely death in 1974, progress in all of Ethiopia would have been even greater. Until Eritrea united with Ethiopia as its motherland, not one Eritrean had graduated from high school or college; a fourth grade education was the limit.

are preparing their own destruction? It is us today, it will be you tomorrow." World War II followed.

He returned to Africa with British help in 1940, with Europe lying prostrate under the Nazi heel, and by 1941 had helped to organize an army of Ethiopians and British that fought their way back to Addis Ababa where he reclaimed the throne.

When the war finally ended in 1945, Haile Selassie's words of wisdom about collective security were uppermost in the minds of world leaders as they met in San Francisco to fashion a new international body called the United Nations—this time, they hoped, one that would practice what it preached. The Emperor of Ethiopia had become a force for the pursuit of world ideals as well as the progenitor of those ideals at home.

With Eritrea restored as part of the Ethiopian nation, once again giving the country access to the sea, Emperor Haile Selassie launched a building program for a merchant marine and opened a naval college to provide military strength at sea. For the army he established a military academy to train its officers, modernized its equipment and organization, and supported it with an air force led by well trained and dedicated pilots and tactical staff.

Today Eritrea is an independent country. Complaints that Ethiopia administered it unfairly are frequently voiced. To straighten the record, I feel I should inject here the fact that until Eritrea united with the Ethiopian motherland, not one Eritrean had graduated from high school or college. Those who were fortunate had a fourth-grade education. In 1972 a total of 95,676 Eritreans were enrolled in secondary school or college, more than for any other province except Addis Ababa, according to a report from the Ethiopian Statistics Authority (Table 1). If statistics were available for 1974, the last year under Emperor Haile Selassie's rule, they would be even more impressive.

The Emperor's drive toward modernization covered many fronts. For the first time in its modern history, he gave the nation its own currency and set up a national bank to oversee fiscal policies. Other important financial institutions arrived on the scene: The National Bank, The Commercial Bank, The Development Bank, The Addis Ababa Bank, Banco di Roma and Agricultural and Industrial Development Bank. Another first: a fine dependable international commercial airline, Ethiopian Airlines, began service around the world.

Ethiopia's rising importance in world government was also manifested by its leadership in creating the Organization of African Unity and in accepting the OAU's wish to have its headquarters in Addis Ababa, which also became the home of the United Nation's Economic Commission for Africa.

Haile Selassie was at the forefront of activities that led to the gradual decolonization of nearly all African states, and he put his collective security principles to work by sending an Ethiopian detachment to help the United Nations subdue aggression in Korea. He came to be looked upon by the people of other African states as their *de facto* leader—loved as much as respected.

Even at home, the Emperor's popularity was sufficient to build a fire under the recalcitrant Rases who ruled the provinces, forcing them to gradually accept the federalism he advocated as the pathway to true nationhood.

The central government became the Ethiopian government in fact, not just on paper. A new constitution was adopted, along with a revamped parliamentary system. More than two million students were enrolled in secondary schools. Higher education at home became possible with the creation of the The University College of Addis Ababa and later Haile Selassie I University (which was later renamed Addis Ababa University by the military government that followed the fall of the Emperor from power) with several branch colleges throughout the country.

Ethiopia slowly improved its ability to manufacture the goods needed by any modern society—textiles, steel, building materials, electrical equipment, paper products, chemicals, printing presses, shoes, and leather goods, among others. And make no mistake about it, Ethiopia aspired to become a modern state, albeit without sacrificing its centuries-old traditions deriving from an agrarian existence.

Food became an industry, no longer just grown and consumed by the growers, but shipped to processing plants for canning, drying, freezing, packaging, distribution at home and shipping abroad. Production of this type rose from less than $30 million (Ethiopian) in 1955 to more than $140 million by 1970. Similar advances were recorded in other industries:

Beverages, from $9.8 million to $63 million

Tobacco, from $4 million to $12 million

Textiles, from $39 million to $180 million

Shoes and leather products, from $4 million to $45 million

Wood products, from $2 million to $20 million

Paper products, from nothing to $12.6 million

Building materials, from $5 million to $38.5 million

Printing and publishing, from $1 million to $10.5 million

Chemicals, from $950,000 to $70.4 million

Metals and electrical products, from nothing to $106 million.

These gains were made through three five-year development plans initiated by Haile Selassie. The fourth five-year plan, which would have ended in 1975, was cut short by the sudden overthrow of the government, and the figures disappeared in the bureaucratic maw of Mengistu Haile Mariam and his successor governments.

Mengistu rose up through the ranks of the Ethiopian Army, starting as a non-commissioned officer and later serving as a major in the military depository at Harar, the provincial capital in eastern Ethiopia, about 500 kilometers from Addis Ababa.

In 1974 a group of so-called intellectuals together with a cadre of ungrateful army officers led by Mengistu conspired to overthrow the government, and did so. At the time of the military *coup d'état,* Mengistu had been chosen by his group of officers to represent them in Addis Ababa in the military committee known as the Dergue. And with good reason.

Mengistu was a consummate actor in the tradition of all dictators who convince their colleagues that they are concerned for the welfare of the state and use their guile to usurp leadership. The men who selected him were useless yes-men of the Soviet Union.

Joseph Stalin was the first "communist" dictator to demonstrate that neither God nor an invading force was needed to eliminate portions of the population that he considered unworthy of life. He slaughtered or deliberately starved more than 25 million people before World War II.

Adolf Hitler refined Stalin's strategies to rid the world of his unwanted millions, as did Pol Pot in Cambodia.

Mengistu was Ethiopia's monster, whatever title he may have bestowed upon himself. From 1974 to 1990 Mengistu ruled with cruel abandon, making history as Ethiopia's first full-fledged dictator and, worse, the cruelest despot ever to rule Ethiopia. Nobody knows or ever will know the number of Ethiopians Mengistu murdered. He and his cadre tried to destroy the Christian religion in Ethiopia, a system that had flourished for nearly 2,000 years. Ethiopia continues to suffer today from the poison Mengistu planted in all fields of Ethiopian life, including human rights, social and religious practice, political policies, and the economy.

These wilful military despots justified their action as necessary to speed up reform. The reforms they sought, however, were not those promoting more freedom for individuals, better educational institutions, or a system with political leaders representing the majority of the people but came directly from political bibles that had guided the Soviet Union. They ended a revolution supporting the people and began one that subjugated the people. Human rights, politics, society, and religion have been devastated, leaving hunger and destitution in the wake of unspeakable exploitation and terror.

Emperor Haile Selassie died in 1975 under circumstances that leave little doubt that he was assassinated. His accomplishments brought Ethiopia out of medieval feudalism into the modern world of productive agriculture, diversified industry, universal education, individual freedom and national dignity. That his successes were sometimes slow in being realized should not detract from his place in Ethiopian or world history. His name will still glow in the world's long-term memory while the identities of modern tyrannical bosses will exist only in a few bloody paragraphs in the story of Ethiopia.

There has been very little increase in industry in Mengistu's Ethiopia, though most of the prerequisites for a broad expansion of domestic consumer goods production and export opportunities had been created by 1974. Internal private initiative and foreign investment have been discouraged by nationalization of production, socialist rhetoric, internal violence, the Somali War and addiction to Soviet-style development policies. At best, industrial production has stagnated. When the facts are known, this author is convinced that it will be found that Ethiopian industry has lost ground during the last 22 years.

What industries have fared best under communist regime? It is ironic that the most successful economic enterprises in Revolutionary Ethiopia since 1974 have been autonomous state corporations established in the imperial era with Western advice and support. These enterprises, standing in bold relief on a decaying economic landscape, included the electric power authority, the telecommunication authority, the cement industry above all, and Ethiopian Airlines.

Since these organizations already belonged to the state, they could not be nationalized but continued to operate according to the principles of management prevailing in Western private enterprises. Providing essential services, they have been able to resist regime interference and continue to perform up to world standards. Since the country's most productive economic activity takes place underground, abandonment of ineffective government controls and proclamation of broad free market principles may enable Ethiopia to recover economic good health more rapidly than estimates based only on official statistics may indicate.

Though the industrial mess created by the communist regime is not as dramatic as the one it made in agriculture, because it has not led directly to starvation and death, it is serious enough to require the post-revolutionary generation to spend untold years in a great effort to catch up to where we were in 1974.

Italian war prisoner General Ablertoni. In 1898 when Italy shamelessly came to Ethiopia to take over the country, Ethiopians taught the Italian soldiers an unforgettable lesson. The brave God-fearing Ethopians defeated the Italians by killing 6,000 soldiers and imprisoning another 4,000.

2

WAR IN THE EMPIRE

The evil clouds of war loomed heavy in the autumn of 1895. The Ethiopian Army had only recently driven out the Italian Army that had advanced over 150 kilometers into Northern Ethiopia, occupying the towns of Adigrat, Makale, and Ambalage.

News of the invasion circulated throughout the Empire, and Emperor Menelek II reported from the capital at Addis Ababa that fresh Italian troops and arms were arriving weekly at the Port of Massawa on the Red Sea. The purpose: not only to re-invade but also to conquer the entire Empire. All Ethiopia was preparing for war.

Gebrie Jire, who had grown into a tall, muscular giant of a man, had reached the age of eighteen. As the son of a balabat and a warrior he was eager to prime himself for the impending war He comprehended the underlying reasons for the war as he had been weaned on the causes.

Many times during his youth he was required to sit silently and listen while his father discussed and debated with the elders of the village of Logahaik the events of the day and yesterday. It appeared that some nation was forever scheming to invade and conquer Ethiopia.

He had heard that in the fourteenth, fifteenth, and the sixteen centuries the aggressors were from the Moslems in the South who warred on religious grounds to change the Empire from a Christian to an Islamic religion. And in this, the nineteenth century, the invaders came from the Mahadi and the colonial powers of Europe.

The village elders would frequently discuss, debate and analyze the issues of the times, particularly how they affected the Empire. There had been discussions on the Suez Canal, which resulted in rerouting the ships from Europe to India through the Mediterranean and Red Sea, thus cutting the distance some 6,000 miles. The elders felt that this event was the beginning of the problems of the Empire, and that the colonial power-hungry European countries were seeking strategic locations all along the East Coast of Africa.

Ethiopians place great significance in Biblical accounts mentioning Ethiopia, including the New Testament (Acts 8:27-40). In the Ethiopian and Israelite chronicles and the reference in the New Testament, the Queen of Sheba who visited King Solomon of Israel (I Kings 10:1-13) was an Ethiopian queen who ruled lands as far east as India from her home country.

Ethiopians believe that Menelek I, son of Solomon and the Queen of Sheba, brought the sacred Ark of the Covenant to the Church of Mariam at Axsum in northern Ethiopia, where it has been preserved through the centuries. From this place, the holiest sanctuary in Ethiopia from the perspective of the 15,000 churches throughout the Ethiopian Empire, word quickly spread of the Italian invasion. Ethiopians of all persuasions—Moslems, Christians and heathens, slaves, peasants, and noblemen—united behind Emperor Menelek II to defend the Empire. Among Christians the word quickly spread: "The Mother of Jesus has come to help the Empire."

The Ethiopians were prepared. For weeks prior to the invasion, sentinels had reported military buildup of the Italian

Army on Mount Enticcio on the borders of Eritrea, the northern Ethiopia region that includes the Red Sea coast. (The original Ethiopian name for this region was Bahre Negash, "Sea of the King." Eritrea is an Italian name.)

An encampment was reported of over 25,000 Italian soldiers, officers and Eritrean *askaris*, a Latin term for people who join the enemy to fight their own country. Reports had also filtered back of the large quantity of cannons, artillery, ammunition and guns.

In preparing for this invasion an Ethiopian army of over 100,000 warriors extracted from all provinces of Ethiopia except Eritrea, which had already been occupied by Italians, prepared to greet the invaders. The defending forces set up camp at Adowa, a small town in the Ethiopian province of Tigre, about 20 kilometers south of the invading Italian camp.

For weeks they had been in training with their cavalry and foot soldiers using their spears and shields and a limited supply of guns, ammunition, cannons, and artillery.

My grandfather Kegnazmuch Gebrie Jire, then a strong young man of 19, was at the Battle of Adowa, supervising the training of cavalry from Wollo. Their warriors practiced battle games and techniques over the vast and foreboding mountainous terrain of black volcanic rock. They felt that their muscles and minds were tuned to fight for months, even years, to defeat the invaders—in spite of the opposition's superiority in weaponry.

I learned about Gebrie Jire from my father and my father's mother and have chosen to include him in this account because I believe he personified the experience and patriotism of Ethiopians.

Gebrie Jire could never forget the piercing sound of the trumpet at dawn on that Sunday morning, March 1 1896, announcing the advance of the Italian army. Troops had crossed the border of Eritrea and were five kilometers inside Ethiopia, headed south towards Adowa.

Although the Ethiopians had anticipated the invasion, they did not expect it to come that day. It was beginning of the Christian Easter season and the time of the feast, a time when all Christians, both Italian and Ethiopian, should have been commemorating the resurrection of Jesus. The *Abuna* (the bishop, or head of the Ethiopian Orthodox Church) explained that the Italians felt that they would take the country by surprise as they had expected the entire country would be in a state of celebration. Additionally, it would be to the Italians' advantage to begin the war during the dry season, before the onset of rains in May and June.

The red-cloaked Ethiopian cavalry quickly prepared for battle. The Italians were advancing unheeded towards Adowa. As the Italian forces approached the outskirts of the town, cannons and artillery fire echoed throughout the mountain passes and valleys overlooking the five churches of Adowa.

The civilian population scurried to safety in their homes. All preparations for the feast were quickly abandoned. The roads of the town were deserted except for the warriors.

Return fire from the Ethiopian army began instantly. All morning turmoil reigned with the staccato burst of machinegun fire mingling with the rapid clack of horses' hooves on rocky soil, the piercing sounds of human cries of wounded and dying, and the harsh metallic clash of shields and swords. Sudden and violent death was everywhere. The body of an Ethiopian warrior shot dead while on horseback lay near an oak tree. Foot soldiers fought their counterparts in vicious hand-to-hand combat in a duel of death. The cavalry fought from horseback with guns and spears. The bodies of the dead, dying and wounded dotted the earth. The rocky, black terrain of Adowa ran with the blood of man and beast. All morning the battle raged. By noon the tide of battle had turned in favor of Ethiopia with over 4,000 Italian prisoners taken and 6,000 Italians killed.

2. War in the Empire

The battle continued in the calm breeze of the Sunday afternoon. The Ethiopian cavalry were successful in separating and isolating the Eritrean brigade. An Italian general was killed, and thousands of Italian and Eritrean prisoners were captured. Later that afternoon, the Italian cavalry abandoned the war and galloped north towards Eritrea and safety.

Through the turmoil, battle cries and cacophony of sounds piercing the air, Gebrie Jire observed Emperor Menelek II sitting motionless on his horse from his hilltop vantage point, watching the battle through binoculars as the assault of the enemy formation raged in the field below. Gebrie and the other loyalist soldiers were inspired by the fact that the Emperor himself lined up with his warriors on this battlefield of death. The presence of their leader bolstered the men to fight with new energy to defeat the enemy.

Gebrie Jire led his victorious cavalry the 200 kilometers back to his home province of Wollo. Over his red cloak he wore a mantle woven in gold and silver, a memento awarded by the Emperor for bravery in war. The return route through the towns of Makale, Sakota, and Magdala were lined with civilians erupting in a festive parade of appreciation for the conquering heroes. It was still the beginning of the same Easter season that had been interrupted by the ominous Italian invasion. Throughout all towns and villages there breathed an euphoric and electrified atmosphere of thanksgiving, praise and gratitude.

The Ethiopian flag of green, yellow and red fluttered everywhere amid sounds of victory songs, resounding drums and the spontaneous clapping of human hands. It was a time of celebration. Straw torches flared throughout the region as the people danced, brass bands played, and the priests and elderly people prayed and thanked the Mother of Jesus for leading the country to victory at Adowa.

Food and drink were plentiful with long tables piled with bowls of *doro wet* (chicken stew), *alecha, kitfo* (raw chopped beef with spices), *yataklete kilkil* (fresh vegetables with garlic and ginger), *talla,* pineapples, coffee and other delicacies of all descriptions.

The cavalcade of rejoicing humanity of all classes united over the defeat of a common enemy must have been an inspiring scene to the Ethiopian war heroes.

On his return from the war front to his home town of Loghaik in the province of Wollo, Gebrie Jire and his warriors became instant celebrities. His father, the warrior of the town, summoned the elders to a meeting so that they could hear first hand the details of the battle that resulted in victory at Adowa. Eagerly they assembled.

Young Gebrie, who had always been required to listen to the debates of the elders, became the center of attention as he related the details of the battle and the subsequent victory. His father was proud of the achievements of his eighteen-year-old son. "You left a boy and returned a man, all in the course of less than a month," he told him.

In recognition of his military success at Adowa, Gebrie was assigned a more active role in assisting his father in the administrative duties of the town of Logahaik.

New developments were in the wind. Emperor Menelek II began pursuing plans to modernize Ethiopia. The Emperor wanted to industrialize the country while at the same time retaining the qualities of life and traditions that were uniquely Ethiopian. He felt this change was necessary in order to avert future confrontations from foreign countries.

The first issue addressed was the development of strategies and laws to abolish small pockets of sporadic customs of slavery within the country. The Emperor had become acutely aware of the rhetoric of some European diplomats who used the issue of slavery in Ethiopia as a pretext to justify their colonialism-inspired aggression toward Ethiopia. Ironically, most of these countries had participated in kidnapping and enslaving African citizens to work in their colonial settlements in the New World. Moreover, the Emperor was aware people in many states of America had held slaves as recently as thirty years before, even after having engaged in a bloody civil war.

In 1897 discussions centered around the purposes for the Treaty of Friendship signed in Addis Ababa between Ethiopia and Great Britain. More discussions and suspicions came from the sudden arrival of foreign diplomats from Russia, Turkey, France, Italy and Sudan to Menelek's court in Addis Ababa. What were these countries up to? Each country appeared to be attempting to develop its own individual interest within Ethiopia. Wisely, Emperor Menelek ignored them to devote his attention to the internal development of Ethiopia.

In the spring of 1898 a tragedy on a hunting trip altered the course of Gebrie Jire's life. He and his friend, Zeleke, were stalking a rare white gazelle in the fields on the outskirts of Logahaik. Zeleke had warned his young friend that to kill such a deer would result in instant death. Gebrie laughed at what he thought was a superstition. He told Zeleke to go to the other side in order to corner the gazelle. Both men were armed with guns as well as spears, but they chose to kill the animal with the spears. Guns were too easy. Among Ethiopians at that time the humble way to kill an animal was by spear. If one missed with the spear, then it was intended that the animal should live.

Gebrie heard a rustle in the tall grass behind him. He turned and threw his spear in the direction of the noise. He hit an unseen object and heard a terrible human cry. Rushing to the spot, he saw Zeleke lying prone, the spear through his breast and bleeding profusely. He died before Gebrie could remove the spear.

For weeks following the funeral of Zeleke, Gebrie Jire grieved. He secluded himself in solitary isolation and became taciturn, speaking only when spoken to. He felt that Zeleke's death was due to his lack of caution despite assurances by his mother and that it was an accident. He withdrew from company of friends, relatives and peers and severed himself from human contact.

As weeks passed there were fleeting moments of recovery as he would emerge from his isolation with sudden good-natured banter only to drift back into his island of loneliness as if the legend of the white deer was haunting him.

One evening after eating a full meal chased with honey wine, Gebrie emerged from his solitude and became very talkative. His father felt encouraged over this sign of recuperation. Gebrie announced that he was going for a ride in the moonlight on Zeleke's horse. His father watched as he mounted the horse and rode away in the moonlight and vanished over the distant hill. Gebrie never again returned to his home.

In 1898 Ethiopian travelers did not worry about food or shelter while traveling throughout the country. It was considered unethical to turn a stranger away from one's door and equally impolite to charge them money for food and shelter. Gebrie had traveled many miles in his early days and had relatives and friends in many provinces. For these reasons he knew he could travel at will throughout the country.

After visiting friends and relatives for several months he visited the Fetewrary Habte Mikael whom he had met at the battle of Adowa. Fetewrary Habte Mikael lived in and administered the Bulga district in the Province of Shoa. An elderly gentleman, he greeted Gebrie with open arms, remembering his bravery at Adowa. He took the former warrior under his paternal wing and invited him to accompany him to meet people, to go on hunting trips and to sit in on sessions as required in carrying out the normal administrative routines of the district. Habte Mikael had only one child, a daughter, Desta, who was twelve years old when Gebrie arrived to become an extended member of the family.

2. War in the Empire

According to the Western Calendar, in the year 1900 (1893 in the Ethiopian calendar, which has a seven-year lag), young Gebrie had reached the age of twenty-three, two years after his arrival at the home of Habte Mikael. One day the Fetewrary told Gebrie that because his duties of administrating the Bulga district had become more demanding with mounting responsibilities and because he was getting old, Fetewrary Habte Mikael offered Gebrie the position of Administrator over a part of the Bulga called Lumè in the province of Shewa. Habte Mikael also stated that he expected Gebrie to marry his daughter Desta, who by then had reached the marriageable age of fourteen. Gebrie Jire agreed to both offers.

The time for marriage is a milestone in the life of young Ethiopians. The parents of both the bride and groom are deeply involved in the decision-making process as well as the ceremony in order to insure that ancient customs and traditions are faithfully followed.

Unlike in the Western world where young men and women are expected to fall in love and court each other prior to making a marriage vow, young Ethiopians often do not meet each other until their wedding day. Tradition and custom dictate that the selection of a marriage partner must be made by the parents of both the bride and the groom.

There are two basic types of prearranged marriage customs. The first type involves an arrangement between two parents that are close friends. If the first set of parents already has given birth to a son and the second set of parents are about to give birth, the pregnant woman is asked to promise that if the child is a female she will become the wife of the infant son. The children therefore have no voice in the selection process.

The second type of arrangement is more complex. When a son reaches a marriageable age, the parents begin looking for a fiancee by searching for a girl whom they consider will be a proper wife.

In the search for the proper wife the parents' selection is based upon the following requirements:

1. She must behave.

2. Her parents must be respectable people.

3. There should be no divorce history in her family.

4. There should not be any serious illnesses in her family.

5. There should be no history of alcoholism or adultery in her family.

6. There should be no history of leprosy in her family.

All the above requirements are investigated by the son's parents prior to proceeding on any steps for marriage. If all these requirements are positive, then the son's parents elect three elderly people to act as witnesses. These three witnesses visit the girl's parents.

The scenario for the elders' visit often proceeds as follows: One morning, quite unexpectedly, the elders would visit the home of the girl's parents. There might be a dog outside that would bark if the father is wealthy, or he might have a servant who would wake him up and announce, "Ababa, three people are outside to see you."

Such a visit is ordinarily made for one of only two purposes. Either a close friend or relative has died somewhere and the elders have come to inform him of the death or if the father has a girl of marriageable age, the elders have arrived to ask for the hand of his daughter in marriage. The father does not know why the elders are paying him this visit.

The father enters the room and asks the elders to sit down. If the elders begin to talk about the weather, the condition of his livestock, or the appearance of his dwelling, the father understands that they did not come to convey news of a death but to ask for his daughter's hand in marriage. He then offers them coffee and breakfast. The elders stand before accepting the offer, and one might say. "We will ask you some questions. If you are in agreement, we will take your offer."

Another elder might begin talking about how respectful his family is and then explain to him that they have a friend who has a son whom they would like to marry his daughter. The wife of the girl's father will then be introduced. They will sit and have breakfast. The wife will then be informed of the purpose of the visit.

Ethiopian mothers always want their daughters to get married, but they want her to marry into a good family. The mother might smile but not make any commitment. Instead, she would arrange a second appointment with the elders by saying, "We will discuss this matter and let you know."

The girl's parents will then begin an investigation of the boy's parents in the same manner. If everything is agreeable, when the elders arrive at the home of the girl's parents for the second visit, they will be informed that the parents are in agreement with the marriage.

All through this investigation neither the boy nor the girl is aware of what is being planned for their future. The parents arrange the marriage date and send invitations to friends and relatives.

When Habte Mikael offered his daughter Desta in marriage to Gebrie Jire neither custom was strictly followed. However, Habte Mikael did base his selection for his daughter on his previous knowledge and present observance and relationship with the young warrior from Wollo.

Desta was my grandmother, and I remember her well. Even in her declining years, she was a beautiful woman. I can only imagine how she must have appeared at the age of fourteen at the time of her marriage to my grandfather, Gebrie Jire, in 1900.

Desta undoubtedly had seen him many times as he had been constantly in the company of her father, Habte Mikael, but probably had no idea that he would become her future husband. Most Ethiopian brides do not become aware that they are about to be married until three days prior to the ceremony. She realizes what is happening when she is put on a fast, given laxatives to weaken her resistance, and required to shear her fingernails. When such requirements are met, Ethiopian girls know that within three days they will be married.

Desta and Gebrie Jire were married at Desta's father's house on a Sunday in a ceremony officiated over by a priest. Desta was a beautiful bride dressed in the Ethiopian white national wedding dress covered with a cloak of gold and blue. Gebrie Jire was resplendent in a *shema,* the Ethiopian national dress, and a dark brown kaba. The bride wore a *homan* (hat) made of golden fabric, the groom a black hat.

Guests came from all over Ethiopia. Gebrie's father and mother arrived from Loghaik for a "mixing day" for the families of the bride and groom. The third day of the wedding festivities, Gebrie presented the required dowry to Desta consisting of gold, diamonds, dresses and perfume. The marriage was consummated while the guests were present, singing, dancing and eating. The maid of honor emerged from the wedding chamber holding a white cloth stained with blood, confirming the virgin purity of the bride. Today, as in the past, virginity at the time of marriage is of paramount importance in the Ethiopian tradition. The guests rejoiced and sang. Desta had passed the test. She was a virgin.

3

GOVERNING THE BALÉ GOBA

In 1900, the year of Gebrie's marriage, his father-in-law, Fetewrary Habte Michael, informed him that Emperor Menelek II had arrived in the province of De Bo Gojo and had requested an audience with Gebrie. Following the war at Adowa, Gebrie had been decorated by the Emperor with the mantle of gold and silver for his bravery. He had not seen the Emperor since that time.

Gebrie's apprehension about the audience with the Emperor vanished when he learned its purpose. He was presented with the new title of Fetewrary and was appointed as the administrator and protector over the Province of Balé Goba that extended five hundred kilometers south to the Kenya and Somaliland borders. Because of Gebrie's demonstrated bravery at the battle of Adowa and his experience as Administrator of Lumè, the Emperor appointed him to govern Balé, a large province bordering Somalia and Kenya—both of which were occupied by European expansionist colonial powers at the time, making his task more difficult.

Such an appointment and the subsequent relocation required many alterations in the lives of Gebrie and his new bride, Desta. A retinue of assistants had to be selected along with servants to oversee day-to-day household tasks. A huge accouterment of supplies, tents, horses, mules, donkeys and apparel had to be assembled and packed to support the entourage during the long journey south to their final destination about 500 kilometers away in the city of Goba Gineer along the river Wabeshebele, one of the great rivers in Ethiopia.

The Balé Goba region in the early 1900s had no roads that were passable with wagons drawn by horses. Travelers to the region had to rely upon horses, mules or donkeys to journey through the vast area. In addition, the custom for a new Fetewrary was that such an individual should not rely on local people for housing and shelter. Custom also required that on their journey within the region they would pass ample time in the villages and towns to meet and greet the local priests, Muslim priests, sheiks, and elders to obtain and understand the conditions existing in each locality.

Emperor Menelek II had apparently outlined to Gebrie the strategic importance of maintaining the integrity of the southern border and protecting it from the encroachment of European countries. With the exception of Ethiopia the entire continent slipped from African to European rule following the Berlin Conference of 1884. European diplomats carved up Africa like a birthday cake—handing out sections to France, England, Germany, Portugal and Belgium and calling them their new colonial empires.

Now in 1900 the scramble over Africa had apparently ended and with the exception of Liberia, only the empire of Ethiopia remained under African rule. Diplomats from Europe were sitting in the capital at Addis Ababa plotting ways to surmount this last encumbrance and colonize Ethiopia.

The anxiety of the Emperor was based on facts. The Dutch and British were struggling for supremacy in South Africa. British settlers had occupied Rhodesia and Nyzaland. In the west the Ashanti country and the area around the Niger had also become British, while the Congo region had become the private estate of King Leopold of Belgium. On the southern border of Ethiopia, Great Britain had proclaimed the Kenya and Uganda territories its "East African Protectorate" and now in 1900 had begun to build a railroad from Mombassa to the ancient African Lake Nyzana that they had renamed Lake Victoria. The primary mission for Fetewrary Gebrie Jire as administrator and protector over the province of Balé Goba became, therefore, to take all measures to insure that the British did not cross the border stretching 850 to 900 kilometers between Ethiopia and Kenya to encroach upon Ethiopian territory.

After two months of preparation, the *nugusaw gazo* (king's journey) under the leadership of Fetewrary Gebrie Jire proceeded south. The cavalcade consisted of over fifty people mounted on horses and mules, followed by additional horses and donkeys loaded with food, supplies and personal belongings. The journey proceeded at an unhurried pace through this pristine region of green mountains and fertile valleys.

The Balé Goba region of southern Ethiopia has an elevation of about 10,000 feet. It is frequently referred to as the Ethiopian highlands. It is an unspoiled paradise and natural home of many species of animals and birds. There are great herds of kudus, oryxes, zebras, giraffes and elephants. Cheetahs and lions roam the forest. Ostriches and hippopotami are frequently found along the edges of rivers. It is also a major agricultural region for the country. Tea, coffee, barley, wheat, ginger, pepper, tobacco and citrus fruits are grown there, and livestock such as cattle, sheep, goats and horses are raised.

This evergreen region is the home of the Oromos people and is also the place where the legendary statue of Shake Husen, known by some Ethiopians as Emanuel, is located.*

**The legend of Shake Husen or Emanuel relates to a day in time when he was confronted by a person attempting to kill him with a spear. The assailant drew back his spear to strike and immediately froze in midair. A hyena rushed forward with teeth bared to bite Shake Husen/Emanuel. It, too, froze. Today a statue depicting this scene stands between the*

Gebrie Jire took three weeks to complete his "king's journey." En route they stopped at towns and villages where they pitched camp and proceeded to the local churches to talk with the priests and to consult with the *balabats* in each region. They updated them on problems facing the Empire and proposals in process that would affect their region. Afterward they dined and at the break of dawn departed to the next community.

The procession finally arrived in the town of Goba Gineer. Gebrie proceeded to hold the usual conferences, first with the Oromo *balabats* and then with the other citizens. The populace was then summoned to a public meeting. The priest announced to the gathering that Gebrie Jire had been appointed by Emperor Menelek to be the new Fetewrary for the Balé Goba region and that he would live among them in Goba Gineer. The *balabat* gave orders to all people to be prepared to assist in the construction of shelters and public buildings to house the new inhabitants.

It was customary in Ethiopia at that time for all people living in a town to volunteer to build structures to house emissaries of the government. The construction phase was viewed by the people as a festive time, and they willingly accepted the challenge.

The building site was located on four acres of land near the river Wabesheble. Five structures were designed by local traditional architects. While women prepared food and drink to nourish the workers, the project began.

Houses were ordinarily built of wood and stone walls with thatched roofs. The *Gibi,* the governor's village of residence and operations, consisted of the *elfign,* (private living quarters), the *adarash* (the place of reception and meeting place for conferences with officials or for court hearings), the *mesaria bet* (warehouse for guns and ammunition), the *enjera bet* (bakery), *wat bet* (kitchen), *tela bet* (brewery house), *wofch bet* (granary), *beklo bet* (stable) and the *beret* (barracks).

An *elfign* is a large round structure organized around a dining room and reception room. The *adarash* (meeting hall) was the second structure to be built. It is a square-shaped building constructed from stone with a thatched roof where court hearings and public meetings are held. The third structure, a large square building constructed from wood, was built as the servants' quarters.

The *enjera bet* and *tela bet* (kitchen and brewery) was the fourth structure completed. It is a separate building always situated at the rear of the compound to prevent the odors and sounds of the food preparation from filtering into the main house. Also in this building, grain is ground to make *enjeria* (bread), food is prepared and stored, *tej* (honey wine) is made, and *tella* (beer) is brewed.

Finally, a huge barn was completed to house horses, mules, donkeys, equipment, and armaments. All buildings were enclosed with a seven-foot stone wall (*ye cab bet*) and hinged with a massive wooden entry gate at front.

A group of artisans prepared furnishings for the dwellings. Furniture was handcrafted from wood. Cowhides formed the base for the seats and backs of chairs and the base for beds. *Mosobs*, used instead of tables from Biblical times in Ethiopia, were woven from dry grass. All of the artisans took great pride in fashioning the items, creating them as carefully as if they were to be used by them personally.

While the project was in process, Gebrie and Desta lived in their tent, and Gebrie immediately began his duties as Fetewrary of the district, holding court and public hearings under a huge oak tree adjacent to the building site. A month and a half after Gebrie's arrival, the buildings were ready to be occupied. A celebration to mark the end of the construction began. All inhabitants of Goba Gineer prepared for the festivities. Cows and goats were slaughtered. *Enjerea* and *wet* were prepared. *Gombo* (kegs) of *tella* were assembled on a huge mosob under the oak tree. The gathering was blessed by the priests, and Gebrie made a speech thanking the towns people for their work. It was a period of great rejoicing with song and dance while the population feasted on meats, *injeria, wet, tej, tella* and coffee.

The evening of the celebration brought good news to Gebrie. Desta informed him that she was with child, the first beginning of a new generation.

A son born in the spring of 1901 was named Adefris. The birth of Adefris in the first year of the twentieth century of the Gregorian calendar can be perceived as symbolic of a new age unfolding, and the end of the tragic nineteenth century. The nineteenth century had been crammed with dramatic changes not only for Ethiopians but for all mankind. From an Ethiopian perspective it represented one hundred years of bloodshed and conquest affecting the lives of people living in every corner of the planet earth.

Future historians could well look upon the nineteenth century and call it a ravenous century of gluttony and greed. The nineteenth century was the century in which European countries and its settlers embarked upon wars to conquer, dominate and subdue all humanity. The nineteenth century was the time when the Australian aborigines lost their continent to the British who colonized it with convicts deported from England. It was the century that the Indian nations of North and South America lost their two continents to England, France, Spain and Portugal. It was the century that all African nations (except Liberia, which was created in the nineteenth century, and Ethiopia) became protectorates of England, France, Spain, Portugal, Belgium and Germany. It was the century that Queen Victoria of England was proclaimed Empress of India. It was the century where inhabitants on all the islands of the seas came under the control and domination of Europeans.

The nineteenth century was also a century of wars, annihilation and great holocausts. It was the century when native populations in Africa, Asia, South America and Australia that resisted European conquest were destroyed. Not only were there wars against native populations but also wars among European power lords to control the planet earth. Never in the history of mankind had human blood flowed so profusely as it did in the bleeding nineteenth century of conquest.

In Ethiopia the nineteenth century was a period of change in traditional lifestyles—lifestyles that had existed before the birth of Christ. It was also a century of bloodshed and many wars. Ethiopia had never invaded other lands to subdue the inhabitants. All of the nineteenth century wars involving Ethiopia were defensive wars against foreign forces seeking to conquer the land. Ethiopia fought throughout the century from all sides of its borders. There were wars with the Egyptians, the Dervishes, the Italians, and the British. Its warriors—led by their Emperors Theodore the Great, John IV, and Menelek II—were able to defeat the aggressors and maintain the integrity of Ethiopia. At the close of the nineteenth century Ethiopia remained unconquered, and Menelek II was actively engaged in plans to modernize and defend his country to resist future invasions.

Adefris, who would later become my father, was born in the first year of this twentieth century into this restless world of conquest, conflict and change. Although a product of the twentieth century his roots went back thousands of years. What challenges did the future hold for my father, Adefris? How would the Emperor's modernization plans affect his life? Would he be able to modernize and yet maintain the traditional Ethiopian value system?

Adefris was born into a strange new world and century, emerging from a dark legacy left by the nineteenth century of bloodshed.

4

MY FATHER GROWS UP

Children born into a given culture always are expected to follow established mores. Their innocent early years are spent in a family unit where they are tutored in the meaning and purpose of the established religious, social and political order. In Ethiopia at the beginning of the twentieth century, the established religious, social and political order had not dramatically changed for over two thousand years.

The early childhood growth and development of Adefris during his first twelve years followed the traditional Ethiopian pattern that established the mold for his life work. From birth, his future had already been well-defined. As the progeny of Fetewrary (Provincial Governor) Gebrie, Adefris too, would one day become a Fetewrary. As for his father before him, young Adefris's formal education began at the age of six at the Orthodox Church. There he learned to read and write not only in Amaharic but also in Ge'ez, an ancient language, which, like Latin, is used only for written works and church liturgy. In effect, Ge'ez is a dead language.

The educational process was prodigious. Adefris studied religious literature in addition to popular histories, chronicles and traditional homilies. Emphasis was placed on learning about the lives and times of the saints, stories of

Christ, the Virgin and the apostles as well as the fabulous miracles attributed to them. He also learned about the historic period of the glory of king Kebra Negast and became fascinated over the chronicles depicting the beginning of the Ethiopian Kingdom with the Solomon Makeda romance.

From this historically rich and colorful Ethiopian environment my father could easily relate the past with the present because there had been few cultural changes through the centuries. In recent years Ethiopia has received from Western historians derogatory criticism because of its observance of so many holidays. In defense of these festive celebrations, it must be remembered that Ethiopian annals go back to 1000 B.C. In the intervening time the country witnessed many heroic accomplishments that are cause for holidays and celebrations. When Western countries have existed as long as Ethiopia has, they, too, will have as many holidays, feasts and celebrations.

Adefris was fortunate to come of age in time to witness first hand the pageantry of these festive celebrations. The majority of Ethiopian feasts and celebrations are Christian observances called "holy days." Among these days are the feasts of Nativity, St. Michael, Abraham, Isaac, Jacob and Our Lady. Other holidays, also religious in origin, include Christmas, Easter, and Maskal or Holy Cross Day.

Adefris told me that he especially liked the brilliant festival of Maskal (Holy Cross). He described a trip to Addis Ababa with his parents and his participation in the celebration. They journeyed on horseback through fields of yellow Maskal daisies in September to the capital city. The celebration began with a troupe of dancers rhythmically moving to the sound of beating drums. Chanting deacons followed, relating liturgies in the ancient Ge'ez language that retold the story of Maskal so that all could hear. They chanted about the lost cross on which Christ was crucified and related the legend going back to the fourth century when Queen Helena, mother of the Roman Emperor, Constantine, journeyed from Rome to Jerusalem in search of the missing Cross. The song told of her arrival in Jerusalem and how she burnt incense and prayed for guidance, how she bent over a column of smoke and, rising, pointed to the spot where the cross was buried, orated on how jubilant she became, and set a bonfire as a sign of thanksgiving over her discovery—an enormous bonfire so bright that Emperor Constantine saw it glowing from his home in Byzantine.

Following the narrating deacons, a procession of priests and lay dignitaries attired in splendid robes and bearing crosses and urns with burning incense strolled past. Adefris watched their stately march through the streets of Addis Ababa until they arrived at a towering unlit *demera* (bonfire) that earlier in the day he and other men and boys of Addis Ababa had participated in building with sticks and poles. The priests circled the bonfire three times and blessed it. Beneath resplendent parasols followed a procession of priests clad in colorful robes, bearing a cross and moving slowly toward the *demera.* As dusk began to fall, Emperor Menelek appeared. He lit an elongated *chubo* (straw torch), proceeded to the bonfire and ignited it. While the bonfire flared, the emperor returned to his place on a raised throne and observed a parade of torch bearers dressed in white robes, each holding a flaming torch. They were followed by more priests, warriors and brass bands, many holding a burning cross. The Maskal festivities always ended with dancing, singing, and feasting.

During these green years of youth, my father learned to swim in the nearby river Wabe, to ride horseback, to hunt and to master the techniques of self-defense in hand-to-hand combat using shields and swords. He was particularly fond of hunting. The hunting party included Gabble, his father, visiting guests, servants, and himself. On hunting days the party would mount their horses and, armed with shields and rifles, proceed into the lush green forest followed by hunting dogs trained to stalk and retrieve fallen prey. Buffalo and hippopotamus were the primary animals stalked, not so much for their meat as for the utility of their tough skins which, when dried, made excellent shields as well as bases for tables, beds and drums.

On one hunting expedition, Adefris remembered felling a *gureza,* a rare tree-dwelling animal with a black and white mane. It is not a monkey and not an ape, but is similar to both. The gureza is a harmless animal that lives in the wild. In Ethiopian legend it is referred to as the saint of animals because it is believed to pray like humans and fast on Wednesdays and Fridays. The fur of the animal is prized for its beauty, which is hung inside the walls of houses as a prized decoration.

Ethiopia's beloved Emperor Menelek II, predecessor to Haile Selassie.

5

MENELEK II

While Adefris matured into manhood during the first two decades of the twentieth century, a profusion of lavish technological developments were being perfected in the industrialized world. These developments, viewed by Western countries as "advancements," transformed the pace of history and eventually impacted the lives of all mankind.

Since the beginning of recorded history, mankind has lived, worked, and died in their tribal realms and regions, unaware of the world at large. Conflicts with neighboring tribes were fought by hand-to-hand combat and resolved when the stronger tribe defeated the weaker. Gunpowder, which was invented in the fifteenth century and later used as the base for rifles, cannons, shells, bombs and torpedoes, changed the course of tribal warfare. With gunpowder it became possible to destroy an enemy without coming into close contact.

During the "Age of Discovery," gunpowder became the principal weapon to destroy other civilizations and to conquer the land of native peoples that had no knowledge of this new firepower. Without gunpowder, it would have been impossible to conquer foreign lands using traditional hand-to-hand combat.

Technological advancements of the twentieth century ushered in new and revolutionary methods of warfare. The airplane, perfected during the first decade of the twentieth century, was subsequently used for the first time on both sides in World War I for large-scale fighting in the battles of the Verdun and the Somme. Pilots fired pistols, rifles, and machine guns at one another from open cockpits.

The gasoline engine was modified for military purposes in World War I in the production of tanks mounted with cannons and military trucks.

Electrical advancement in the twentieth century also revolutionized communications and made it possible to monitor, send and receive messages quickly regarding the progress of enemy attacks.

In the short span of twenty years, the West leaped forward with these new technologies and looked upon countries that relied upon traditional methods as backward, primitive, barbaric and even uncivilized.

For some years after the Ethiopian victory over the Italians at Adowa, an atmosphere of intense rivalry existed among Britain, France, Germany and Italy to subjugate and colonize Ethiopia. Britain and France felt that as long as Italy remained in Eritrea, she held the balance of power in the region and neither Britain nor France felt strong enough to move against Ethiopia alone. Political rivalry was acute as the governments of Britain, France, Italy, Russia, Turkey, and the Sudanese Derbush sent emissaries to Emperor Menelek's court in Addis Ababa in order to promote their own interests.

In 1906, when my father was still a young boy, a series of secret meetings was held. Ethiopia was excluded. A Tripatrite Treaty was signed by Britain, France and Italy, and the three countries agreed that none of them would "infringe in any way, the sovereign rights" of Emperor Menelek II of Ethiopia, but asserted their "right, in the event of rivalries or internal changes in Ethiopia to intervene to protect their nationals and to act, always in concert, to safeguard their respective interests."

Thus, without the knowledge or consent of Emperor Menelek, these three countries agreed to balkanize Ethiopia, slicing it arbitrarily into three European spheres of influence. To Britain would go the northwestern section of the country in the Gojjam region—including Lake Tana, the source of the Blue Nile. To France would go the east central section of the country from the railway linking their port in French Somaliland at Djibuti on the Gulf of Aden through the Danakil region to Addis Ababa. Italy would receive the territory from the north bordering on their province in Eritrea and extending south past Addis Ababa, connecting to their southeastern territory of Italian Somaliland on the Indian Ocean. This territory would include the Tigre region, part of the Danakil and Kaffa region, and all of the Harar and Ogaden region. As a result of this clandestine treaty of 1906, Italy was promised virtually the whole of Eastern Ethiopia.

Emperor Menelek was incensed when the news of this shocking Tripatrite Treaty reached his ears. He demanded an explanation from the British, French and Italian Ministers stationed in Addis Ababa, bluntly stating his opposition to the treaty. He insisted that for any treaty to be valid it would have to have the consent of all the parties involved, not just the unanimous consent of the beneficiaries.

The clandestine treaty alluded to factors that would give the three countries the "right" to intervene in concert to deal with "frontier incidents," exploitation by "financial advisers, military and religious missions," and "internal disturbances leading to internal changes"—all ambiguously worded to give the ruling countries the right to take military action for virtually any reason.

The Tripatrite Treaty of 1906 created a framework to justify an invasion of Ethiopia by Britain, France and Italy.

Britain and France had become experts during the previous century in creating treaties and fomenting incidents that resulted in their annexing other peoples' lands all over the globe. Until this event, Italy was relatively inexperienced in the arena of empire building.

I am convinced that it was for only one reason that the Tripatrite Treaty was prevented from being implemented. In 1906 Britain and France were heavily involved protecting their interests against other European countries. In 1882 Germany, Austria-Hungary and Italy had signed the Triple Alliance Treaty, which was designed to protect its members against attack by France or Russia. Germany and Italy feared France, while Germany and Austria-Hungary feared Russia.

Then in 1904 Great Britain and France became diplomatic partners, reaching an *entente cordiale* or "cordial understanding" for settling their disputes about colonies. In 1907 Russia joined the two nations with a new agreement called the Triple Entente. This agreement divided Europe into two opposing armed camps. Between 1905 and 1912 France came close to war with Germany several times over disputes on the control of the Morocco region in North Africa.

With all of these issues at the forefront and lacking an international organization to help settle their disputes, both Britain and France were prevented from attempting any conquest of Ethiopia. Italy, which had been defeated by the Ethiopians in the Battle of Adowa in 1898, was reluctant to attempt a new invasion alone. They knew that such a foray would be extremely hazardous because Emperor Menelek had united the people of Ethiopia as no Emperor had previously done.

To the populace the Emperor was affectionately referred to as "Degu Menelek" or "Menelek the Kind-Hearted." He had already restructured his cabinet creating twelve ministers: Ministers of Defense, Palace, Finance, Agriculture, Commerce, Education, Mining, Communications/Telegraph, Justice, Human Re-sources/Development, and Pensions. Menelek had the prestige of a warrior, a status that counts for much in Ethiopia, where every man must be a soldier. He held complete power over his people where he reigned wisely.

Ethiopians did not believe in invading other people's lands, subjugating their people, and colonizing their territories. Nevertheless, when invaded, the people were trained from youth to unite and fight a common aggressor.

Early in his reign, Emperor Menelek developed a standing army as a defensive measure since at the time Ethiopia and Japan were the only countries that had not been destroyed by European industrialization.

In the process of studying the West for its practical lessons, Menelek became increasingly discriminating in his understanding of differences among the many Western countries. He became acutely aware that the more advanced Western countries were undergoing industrialization to modernize their economies, while some European countries had not advanced. Menelek was concerned about how Ethiopia could advance industrially without losing, under the flood of this headlong Westernization, qualities that were uniquely Ethiopian. He felt that Ethiopia needed Western progress only because the country was surrounded by it. Aware that "progress" expediting the industrialization of Ethiopia could become either a benefit or misfortune, he was afraid of being swamped by Western thought.

The rise and fall of nations is strongly allied with the will of their people, and it is the temperament of the people that controls the fate of its people. During his reign, Menelek the Good was instrumental in defeating all common enemies, unifying the people, improving the political hierarchy, instituting industrial changes and organizing a standing army.

The basis for Ethiopian courage can be traced to ancient Ethiopia. The culmination of a country's civilization is not achieved in a day but is conceived several thousand years in advance.

Historical evidence suggests that there are dangers in radical alterations of traditional patterns resulting in social dislocation and confusion. Sudden changes to new things and the abandonment of the old will always produce extreme discomfort in the human heart. Additionally, all countries are characterized by a desire to retain old institutions and practices. There are few if any benefits of forcing people to abandon ancient practices and accepting foreign ideologies and practices.

Choosing to join the Western march of progress would require great caution, adaptation, and selectivity in adopting Western ideologies, techniques and institutions—especially for Ethiopia, whose three thousand years of historical experience was totally alien to the mere four hundred years of experience of the West.

Emperor Menelek II died sometime during the first decade of the twentieth century. The news of his death was kept secret from the populace for several years. Reports from the palace at Addis Ababa stated that "His Majesty is ill." Proclamations and decrees issued in his name by his ministers implied he was still alive.

Speculations over the reasons for the concealment of the Emperor's death are twofold. At the time of his death, Menelek had three direct heirs apparent to the throne: His daughter, Princess Zauditu; his grandson, Abeto Lij Eyassu; and his cousin, the astute Tefri Makonnen, who later took on the name Haile Selassie after he became king. Some believed that at the time of his death, none of the three had adequate knowledge or experience to govern the country and that time was needed to assist them in developing the required skills. Others believed that had the news of the

Emperor's death been disseminated, there would have been an immediate invasion of the country by Britain, France, and Italy. This belief was supported by statements contained in the clandestine Tripatrite Treaty of 1906, which stated that "in the event of rivalries or internal changes," the three countries would invade to protect their interest.

Fortunately for all Ethiopia, the public announcement of Menelek's death was not announced until December 1912—prior to the outbreak of the Western World War I when all the would-be owners of Ethiopian lands were bitterly embroiled in European civil disputes.

Ethiopia did not participate in this European fraternal conflict for three good reasons. First, adversaries from both sides were reputed to be Christian nations, and for Christian nations to engage in battle against each other was considered by Ethiopians to be sacrilegious. Second, during the nineteenth century, Ethiopia had encountered bitter conflicts with Britain, France and Italy over the integrity of Ethiopia's government and was deeply engaged in plans to improve its structure. Finally, Ethiopia was opposed to the arguments from both sides of the European struggle as it strongly involved a colonial conflict which Ethiopia had never supported.

And so, while European countries were actively embroiled in their internal strife to control the destiny of the planet Earth, Ethiopia had time to reflect, to mourn, and to bury their beloved Emperor Menelek II.

My father, Adefris, was eleven years old when the news of the Emperor's death was announced to the public. For the rest of his life he vividly remembered the shock and grief that gripped and paralyzed the land over this heartbreaking announcement. Everywhere Adefris looked, people stood, stunned in disbelief. With streaming tears he heard their moaning lament: "No, not degu Menelek! No, not degu Menelek! No, not degu Menelek!"

For forty days all Ethiopia mourned the departure of Menelek the Good. The doleful sound of beating drums echoed through mountains and valleys throughout the land. Everywhere the populace changed their traditional white cloaks and *chammas* to black in honor of the departed statesman. Women of all classes openly shed grievous tears. Flags on public buildings fluttered at half mast throughout the land as *alkashochs* (mourners) wailed dirges singing praises for their beloved Emperor.

"Menelek the Great at Uccalli!" shouted one in the mountain air.

"Menelek the Great Man at Adowa!" wailed another.

"Menelek the Builder of Addis Ababa!" praised one standing by a tree.

"Menelek the Father of Ethiopian Unity!" exclaimed another from a mountainside.

"Menelek! Oh Menelek! Both Mother and Father of the Nation, have left today!" moaned another bent over in solemn prayer.

The funeral was held at the capitol building Emperor Menelek had established in 1896. Four years earlier, he had looked out from the mountain of Entoto that soared 10,000 feet above the valley. Gazing down upon a vast area shimmering with yellow flowers as if the entire region was encased in a huge natural bowl, he proclaimed, "Addis Ababa!" ("New Flower"). Addis Ababa became the new capital city of Ethiopia in 1896.

My father, Adefris, my grandfather, Gebrie, and my grandmother, Desta, were among the throng of mourners marching to the solemn sound of beating drums. The streets of Addis Ababa swelled with multitudes from all classes, tribes and religious groups. All marched slowly, silently, by the palace where the Emperor lay in state. Sounds of drums, shrill pipe music, and funeral songs filled the very air and seemed to sway with the wind. Bright brass horns flashed and loomed above the heads of the mourning masses blaring traditional songs of state. From every side came priests, monks and deacons, wearing rosaries at their waists. One priest openly exclaimed:

> Cry Ethiopia! Cry Ethiopia! Cry Ethiopia!
> You've lost your beloved son!
> Who tried to make your country great!
> And who did so!
> So, Cry Ethiopia! Cry Ethiopia!

All day long drums beat against the hillsides as priests and clergy chanted eulogies in Ge'ez, and all Addis Ababa wept. When the Emperor's casket was lowered into his grave, the spontaneous sound of singing voices soared throughout all Addis Ababa and Ethiopia.

> "Oh, Ethiopia be happy
> By God's power and your Emperor!"

Lij Eyassu, heir apparent, 1914

6

TURBULENCE STIRS THE WORLD

Within two years after the Ethiopian Emperor's funeral, World War I of the Western world began. Essentially, the war started in July of 1914 as a European tribal conflict among countries speaking different tongues. People sharing a common culture grouped together in rival military alliances to advance their tribal ambitions. These countries competed not only to control European countries but also those countries scattered all over the planet that had been subjugated and colonized by them during the eighteenth and nineteenth centuries. Thus, the Allies, which included Belgium, France, Great Britain, Russia and Serbia, entered into a bloody conflict against the Central Powers of Austria-Hungary, Bulgaria, Germany and the Ottoman Empire. The war that lasted for four years eventually involved other countries that became sympathetic with the Allied causes.

Ethiopia remained aloof from this European family turmoil. Up to that point the traditional Ethiopian attitude toward Europeans had been amicable. Their first close encounter with Europeans was with the Portuguese adventurers, referred to by the Ethiopians as "red" not "white" men. These Portuguese, and the white European Jesuits who accompanied them, were highly esteemed because they assisted Ethiopia in its long and bitter wars against Islam.

The conflict with other European countries that eventually resulted in a deterioration of mutual respect began about 1850 during the time of Ethiopia's Emperor Theodore the Great. The British, under the leadership of their General Napier, invaded Ethiopia supported by an army from Egypt, India and Yemen to rescue so-called hostages. The confrontation continued when the Italians, French and British annexed neighboring lands on Ethiopian borders colonizing them into Eritrea, French Somaliland, Italian Somaliland and British Somaliland.

The climax of this European travail was reached at the end of the century with the defeat of the Italians at Adowa in 1898 when the Italians attempted to conquer and colonize all of Ethiopia.

From 1914 to 1918, while the European World War I was raging, Ethiopia enjoyed a time of peace. It was also a time to install a new head of state after recovering from the bereavement over their recently departed Emperor, the beloved Menelek II.

Throughout the course of recorded history, pharaohs, Emperors, kings and queens reigned supreme over the subjects of their lands. The death of a reigning monarch always implied a hereditary replacement to the throne, particularly if the departed ruler was beloved by his subjects.

Emperor Menelek II was revered by his subjects. He had two daughters, Zauditu and Shewareged. There were no direct male heirs to the throne. His oldest daughter, Zauditu, was childless. However, his other daughter, Woizero Shewareged, had a son, Lij Eyasu, from her marriage to Negus Michael of Wollo. Before his death, Emperor Menelek II nominated his grandson, Lij Eyassu, as his successor to the throne of Ethiopia, and appointed Ras Tessemma as his guardian.

By 1914, the heir apparent, Lij Eyassu, had matured into a tall, handsome and virile young man. He was also a scholar, a visionary, and a liberal who openly declared that he did not wish to become king until all Ethiopia was united. This meant Moslems, Christians, pagans—all classes, poor and rich, all different tribes living in harmony. To prove his progressive intentions, he traveled north, south, east, and west throughout the land proclaiming his new doctrine of unity. In his zeal he defied custom and traditional values and began to have amorous affairs with women regardless of class or other distinctions. A brazen young man, Lij Eyassu fathered many children.

This unseemly behavior shocked the traditionalists of Ethiopia, particularly the Shoan and Tigre nobles, the ruling class of Ethiopia at that time, and Abuna Matteos, the Archbishop of Ethiopia and the real power behind the throne. In his fervor to be liberal, Lij Eyassu had committed the unpardonable sins of ignoring the cultural and moral standards of his people.

Abuna Matteos and his priests concluded that they could never accept the wild Lij Eyassu on the Imperial throne of Ethiopia and began to explore a method of selecting a more acceptable successor whom the country and particularly the Christians could respect. They selected Emperor Menelek's daughter, Zauditu, who would become the first woman to ascend to the throne of Ethiopia since the Queen of Sheba.

Fetewrary Gebrie, his wife Desta and son Adefris journeyed to Addis Ababa and were among the guests witnessing Zauditu's coronation. On September 27, 1916 they were present at the banquet hall of Talaku Gibbe to hear the sonorous voice of Abuna Mateos proclaim Zauditu the Empress of Ethiopia. They also heard him proclaim Ras Taferi Makonnen as heir to the throne and regent. The Abuna warned that "any man who refused to accept both proclamations would incur the wrath of the Father, Son and Holy Ghost, the anathema of the twelve Apostles and 318 Fathers of the Council of Nicaea, and be smitten with the curse of Arius and the reprobation of Judas," and, in conclusion, "with my humble word, I excommunicate him."

Empress Zauditu, peering through powerful, dark eyes set under a broad forehead, accepted both the proclamation and the throne. Though small in stature, she possessed a magnificent and impressive bearing. She had acquired many of her father's mannerisms along with the qualities of tactfulness and shrewdness. When questioned about her height, she was heard to say, "Small I am like Queen Victoria, great like her I hope to be."

My father thus reached manhood during an age of turbulent global disruption caused not by natural calamities but by the unnatural cataclysmic dissolution of the ancient way of life. The European World War I provided the background of turmoil that infected all mankind.

Ethiopia watched the struggle waged on the battlegrounds of Europe, speculating on how the outcome would affect its empire. In 1917 Russia withdrew from the war, Tsar Nicolas II was overthrown in a revolution, and the Bolsheviks seized power.

Did these events foredoom the end of the age of the Ethiopian empire? Who were these Bolsheviks who challenged their own traditional values? Were they made of the same cloth that fashioned the British subjects who overthrew the rule of King George II of England and established a new democratic republic in the American colony? If not the same, they both challenged and overthrew their empires. The Bolshevik force of the new ruler, Nikolai Lenin, took control of all Russian industries, established central management bureaus and secret police, permitting workers to control factories and peasants to seize farmlands.

7

A TIME OF PEACE FOR ETHIOPIA

While Adefris listened attentively to his father's daily discussions of foreign events, it seemed to the young man that life in Ethiopia was tranquil, continuing its traditional patterns without interruption. His encounter with Europeans was minimal. In Addis Ababa he had seen bearded men in the distance, clad in strange costumes. He was told they came from such unknown places as England, France, Sweden, Belgium, Italy and Russia. Occasionally he had seen their pale-skinned women dressed in bizarre clothing and wearing uncomfortable-looking skirts. He had never spoken to any of them, and so their world and the places from where they sprang remained wrapped in mystery.

Above all else, my father Adefris was an Ethiopian, the son of Fetewrary Gebrie Jire of Balé Goba, a province in southwest Ethiopia. Daily he accompanied his father, observing, assisting, and learning the many activities necessary to administer the region. Many issues pressed to the forefront.

The Balé Goba region was primarily pagan, particularly in the provinces of Balé. One of my grandfather Gebrie's missions as the Fetewrary was to expand Christianity's influence and teach its principles to the inhabitants. Six churches were constructed. In Arusi Province the churches of Gololcha, Manga Medanaelem (Church of Jesus Christ), Harrow Giorgis, Worgu Michael and Chole Mariam were organized. In the district of Dara Lebu of the Harrar Province, the church of Daro Michael was established.

In order to minister the churches, Fetewrary Gebrie recruited missionary priests and monks from the provinces of Wollo, Shoa, Gondar and Gojjam. These priests were charged with the responsibility of teaching the people Christian principles. The effects of this religious effort resulted in the conversion of a large portion of the population, not only from paganism but also from Islam to Christianity.

In addition to their religious duties, Adefris and his father Gebrie kept busy with administrative activities. In Balé Goba taxes were levied and collected on grain and livestock. There were administrative duties over the weekly labor pool that was responsible to maintain public roads and buildings and always new rules had to be defined regarding *dergo* (public hospitality). Many ancient laws were based on complex religious, civil and penal interpretation of the Mosaic Law and written in Ge'ez, that had to be assessed and interpreted by priests. These included laws relating to inheritance, divisions of estates, divorce, disputes, women's rights, and crimes of violence.

Peculiar to Ethiopian law are those relating to women and their rights. The word of women is always accepted without witness or guarantee. Judgment is always granted in support of her testimony without additional witnesses. Another peculiarity of Ethiopian law is that relating to murderers. Only the king can impose death sentences. All persons accused of murder are sent to Addis Ababa to be tried, and those found guilty are sentenced to be executed in the districts where the crimes were committed.

7. A Time for Peace for Ethiopia

One day a courier arrived from Addis Ababa. Empress Zauditu had summoned Fetewrary Gebrie and his son Adefris to appear for an audience at the palace in Addis Ababa to receive instructions on a crisis brewing in the Ogaden Region along the Somali border.

As his son I know that Adefris never forgot the trip to the palace at Addis Ababa with his father. He described it for me many times. As they approached upwards on Talaku Gibbe, the great concourse and imperial palace to which all roads seemed to lead, he saw more than one hundred staff members at the entrance to the palace. The sentries at the palace gate were shrouded in hoods and cloaks. Through a succession of irregular, stonewalled yards, Adefris observed riflemen, splendidly trapped mules, servants and officials. An usher waved a long wand to make way for them. The Gibbe covered at least a square mile, and in the center of its maze of courts, nestled among acres of thatch, mud, iron and stone, stood two pavilions with outside staircases and tiered balconies, where Empress Zauditiu lived.

Adefris was excited. He would soon meet Empress Zauditu, daughter of Menelek II the Lion of Judah, Queen of Ethiopia. They were received on the second floor, in an octagonal pagoda-like room, spread with fine carpets. On the wall hung portraits of Menelek II and his wife, Empress Taitu. The only items of furniture in the room were two seats placed for Adefris and his father, and a lower chair on which Empress Zauditu was enthroned with her tiny feet resting on a velvet cushion. Behind her stood her lady in waiting, and on either side stood her chamberlains and priests.

Zauditu was a small woman, but her bearing was impressive. Only her eyes and cheeks were clearly visible between the muffling folds of white silk gauze. Even the hand Adefris touched seemed to be covered in the same white, silky fabric. Her great dark eyes gazed out, intelligent and quiet.

Empress Zauditu gave them a briefing on the crisis brewing on the Somali border. Somali soldiers had entered the Ogaden Region. She believed the invasion was inspired by foreign sources with a mission to drive them from the region She commended Fetewrary Gebrie on his bravery at Adowa and complimented him on his work in establishing churches in the provinces of Arusi and Bale. She then appointed Adefris to lead an Ethiopian cavalry against the Somali invasion in the Ogaden region. After the briefing and a few minutes of talks and blessings, she and her entourage left Fetewrary Gebrie and Adefris to view the town of Addis Ababa from her balcony.

Beyond the palace roofs, the trees dropped to a ravine and climbed again, rank after steel blue rank, backed by the mountain mist. They saw the tiny figure of Empress Zauditu and her entourage pass across the courtyard below, a velvet umbrella fringed green and red held over her head by the lady in waiting and surrounded by a group of courtiers. Lions roared from their cages on one side. Soldiers bared their heads as she passed. Priests chanted near the massive throne room of the Gibbe as rose petals fluttered at her feet.

On their return trip to their home in Balé Goba, Adefris and his father Gebrie discussed the Somali invasion. Historically, they knew, the lands that had recently become French, British, and Italian Somalilands on the Ethiopian eastern border in the mid-nineteenth century were part of the old Ethiopian empire. Tradition states that the name "Somali," which meant, "my left side," was given to the region by the Queen of Sheba and that she named another part of her empire "Yemen" ("my right side") on the same day that she prepared to travel to Jerusalem to visit Solomon.

Territorial divisions between Ethiopia and Somali did not exist before European intervention. Even today the nomadic Somalis enter the Ogaden with their camels, cattle, and goats—free to graze without any formal restrictions.

In the thirteenth, fourteenth, and fifteenth centuries, Ethiopia engaged in an almost continuous religious warfare with the Arabs who invaded the region and were converting the people to Sunnite Moslem beliefs, a branch of Islam.

Conflicts between the Somali and Ethiopian people has always been of a religious nature. The Somali region is situated on the horn of Africa along the Gulf of Aden and the Indian Ocean. It is a hot, dry land peopled by nomadic herdsmen who wander over the region with their cattle, camels, goats and sheep in search of water and pasture.

After the Europeans arrived and balkanized the land into French, British, and Italian Somaliland possessions in the last half of the nineteenth century, the people ignored this intrusion, continuing their pattern of existence and traveling within the three regions as if there were no territorial division.

At the time the area was partitioned, Europeans agreed that the Ogaden region would remain Ethiopian. Having obtained this concession, but doubting the intent of the Europeans to honor the agreement, Ethiopia jealously guarded its territorial border. When Somali soldiers invaded Ogaden, Ethiopians believed this invasion was European inspired. Ethiopia was prepared to fight to drive them out.

The Ogaden region of Ethiopia is a vast grassland region covering over 175,000 square kilometers. Situated in the southeast corner of the country, it is bordered on the south by Kenya, on the east by Italian Somaliland and on the north by British Somaliland. The area is so extensive that both the countries of England and Italy could fit comfortably inside its territory. It was in this region that young Adefris and his cavalry were dispatched by Empress Zauditu to defend their country against the Somali army.

The battle occurred in the Walwal region in the Ogaden where there were over a thousand underground wells that the Somalis sought to control for grazing purposes. Adefris led the Ethiopian cavalry into battle, where they confronted a band of Somali soldiers. Suddenly Adefris's horse, a *tegafi feres* (a horse that cannot be stopped by bridle reins) lunged forward and took him into the midst of the enemy camp, isolating him from his troops. Adefris was surrounded by Somalis. He took his sword and shield and bravely began to fight in desperate hand-to-hand combat. He killed seven Somali soldiers while wounding many more. Finally, his cavalry arrived and entered the battle. Hours later the Somalis fled on their horses back to the Somali border. Ethiopia was victorious. Over two hundred Somalis lay dead on the battlefield, and 127 prisoners had been captured.

Among the prisoners was a young Somali named Ali. He was presented as a gift to my grandfather Fetewrary Gebrie by Adefris on his return to Balé Goba. Fetewrary Gebrie adopted him and gave him the name, Ali Gebrie. Adefris considered Ali to be his own brother and the second son of Fetewrary Gebrie. In later years I knew Ali Gebrie and regarded him as my uncle. He named his first son Haile Selassie Ali. According to Ethiopian custom regarding adopted sons, Ali Gebrie and Adefris became equal heirs to the property of my grandfather, Fetewrary Gebrie Jire.

The sword my father Adefris used to fight to defend his country from foreign invaders in the Ogaden battle and later in the Maichew battle against the Italians was confiscated from my house by Mengistu's scavenger military junta in 1975.

The European World War I ended on November 11, 1918 when the German Secretary of State, Matthias Erzberger, signed an armistice conceding victory to Ferdinand Foch, the General-in-Chief of the Allied Armies in France. This war took the lives of twice as many men as all major wars from 1790 to 1913; in addition, civilian deaths in the war-torn region exceeded five million, many of whom died from starvation, disease or exposure. Spanish influenza, which some blamed on the war, caused millions of other deaths.

In addition to this devastating loss of human lives, the intense bombing and shelling in areas of military operations destroyed the industrial and commercial lives of cities, towns, and villages and closed or destroyed schools, hospitals, factories, roads and railroads, for an overall estimated cost of over 350 billion dollars.

Of particular interest to Ethiopians as the War came to an end was the Treaty of Versailles signed by the defeated Germans. This agreement declared that Germany was solely responsible for the European World War I. As punishment, the treaty took away all the colonies of Germany, divested the country of its overseas investments and established the League of Nations. This treaty, which was signed in the Hall of Mirrors in the Palace of Versailles near Paris on June 28, 1919, stripped Germany of her African colonies and created a mandated system administered by the League. The League expected governing countries to improve conditions for the people in the mandated territories and to prepare the people in the territories for self-government.

The colonies in Africa that were lost by Germany as a result of the Treaty of Versailles included Tanzania, which was mandated to the British; parts of the Cameroons and Togoland, which were mandated to the French; Ruanda-Urundi, which was mandated to the Belgians; and German South West Africa (now Namibia), which was mandated to the Union of South Africa. The League of Nations appointed a commission to supervise the mandate system. The commission had no power to govern, but was generally successful in persuading nations with mandates to improve education, public health, and the economy.

Empress Zauditu and the Regent, Ras Tefri Makonnen, delegated the Foreign Minister of Ethiopia, Blattengueta Herouy Wolde Selassie, to attend the peace treaty negotiations at Versailles and to return with information on the new League of Nations. Foreign Minister Blattengueta Herouy, a multilingual writer, was one of the most widely traveled and highly respected of all Ethiopians at that time. In addition to being Foreign Minister, he had been the Kantiba (mayor) for Addis Ababa and chief editor of the newspaper Berhnena Selam. He represented Ethiopia at the coronation of King George V of Britain in 1910. He spoke many languages—including Amaharic, Arabic, French, Russian, and English—and was held in high regard by his colleagues.

He returned from Versailles with the news that the League Covenant contained articles in which member nations pledged to preserve the independence of member countries and to defend the territory of all members against attack. Members also agreed to submit any disputes that might lead to war to arbitration or to an investigation by the League Council. Ethiopia did not rush in to join the League of Nations in spite of the fact that over forty other nations had joined and that the articles of the League favored a system of collective security guaranteeing protection for all members.

Ethiopia's opposition to joining the League came from Empress Zauditu herself, followed by the governors of the provinces and the priests of the Ethiopian Orthodox Church. Ethiopia had always been isolationist and nonaligned with other nations. Prior to the recent European War, the country had felt threatened by the new colonies of France, Great Britain and Italy established on its borders, and now all three had agreed to the principals of the League Covenant and had become members. Ethiopia remained suspicious. In the words of Habte Giorgis, Ethiopia's Minister of War, "Ethiopia does not wish to fall under the evil eye of the foreigner."

The early 1920s continued as a period of peace and calm in Ethiopia. While debates about the propriety of becoming a member of the League of Nations were being published, Fetewrary Gebrie Jire and his wife Desta announced the betrothal of their son Adefris to Likelesh Gebresilasie in 1922.

Likelesh was well educated and although she was among the first Ethiopian women to study at the French school in Harrar, she was a traditionalist and a devout Christian in the Orthodox Church. Likelesh's father, Fetewrary Gebresilasie, and her mother, Weletmikael Geligto (Minjeche), announced the betrothal in the presence of Adefris' father and mother, Fetewrary Gebrie Jire and Desta, who were to serve as grantors. When this was confirmed by oath in the name of the priest, the engagement became binding.

On their wedding day, Adefris had reached the age of 23; Likelesh was fourteen. She was a tall beautiful bride cloaked in the traditional Ethiopian shamma, her delicate features veiled in white silk muslin.

The wedding proceeded as weddings had for thousands of years. Adefris presented his dot (dowry) of clothes, jewelry, perfume and words of promise to his bride, proving himself to be a responsible man who would respect her rights. A gala banquet followed with Ethiopian music, chatting and dancing by the friends and relatives. It was a happy day. A time of peace. A time to marry. A time to pray. A time of innocent youth unfolding, unaware that this would be counted one of the happiest days of their lives. From this day they headed into a future laden with drastic changes. Peace would be destroyed, and war and death would reign supreme.

Empress Zauditu, Ethiopia's first ruling woman since the Queen of Sheba.

8

LEADING ETHIOPIA TO NEW HEIGHTS

Early in 1923 Empress Zauditu was finally persuaded to submit Ethiopia's application for membership to the League of Nations, in spite of opposition by the governors of the provinces and priests of the Church. Ethiopia was accepted as a member in September 1923, supported by their former enemy, Italy and receiving opposition from only one country, Great Britain.

With the elimination of the threat of future encroachment and wars by foreigners, Ethiopia enhanced its pace of internal changes. The chief protagonist for change was the regent and heir to the throne of Ethiopia, Ras Teferi Makonnen, who would assume the name of Haile Selassie upon his coronation.*

**Haile Selassie's given name was Teferi Makonnen. Later he carried the title Ras Teferi (Ras is the Ethiopian eqnivalent of Field Marshall). When he was crowned Emperor he was given the coronation name of Emperor Haile Sellasie. In Ethiopian tradition people are given new names to correspond with titles of prominence when they are appointed to the positions of Archhishop or Emperor.*

On the whole the heir to the throne tended not to interfere with the established governors unless they resisted changes he considered necessary. Ras Teferi Makonnen felt the governors and nobles were too powerful to overthrow and that it would be folly to alienate them. He hoped in time they might be persuaded to assist him in making peaceful changes. He was not a warrior like the former Emperors—Theodore II, John and Menelek—and, like the people of Western countries, Ethiopians respected warriors and physical force.

But Haile Selassie excelled over the others in one trait: his intelligence. From his school days at the French Catholic Mission in his native Harar he had been exposed to Western culture, from his parents he inherited the graces of authority, and the knowledge of Ethiopians gave him the insight to maneuver diplomatically for internal change.

The problem confronting Haile Selassie was twofold: to give Ethiopia internal stability and also to make her powerful enough to withstand outside pressures from foreigners. He strongly felt that the provinces that were still divided had to be welded into a single homogeneous state. Other countries he had studied had faced the same problem. England had problems with the Irish, Welsh and Scots. Italy had been governed by foreigners until union came in 1861, and the United States of America was divided between north and south. It became clear to Haile Selassie that the key factor to growth and prosperity for all these countries had been unity. Internal division among the provinces was a luxury Ethiopia could ill afford.

Even prior to Ethiopia's admission to the League, Haile Selassie reaffirmed an edict of Menelek II against the slave trade: "Any person is liable to the death penalty who, without the King's authorization and except in case of war, seizes any person by violence with the object of enslaving him."

The ruler's intent to enforce this provision was soon affirmed by the public execution of several dealers who were caught contravening the slave laws. Their bodies were hung at the gateways of their native towns to serve as a grim warning of the dangers of defying the government.

Another edict against the slave trade was issued by Empress Zauditu in 1924. She proclaimed that any slave who could "prove cruelty or underfeeding against his master; who had been sponsored by their owners at baptism; who with their owner's permission had entered the Army or Church; and any slave whose master had not claimed him within a week of an arrest," would be liberated. Further clauses in the same decree provided that slaves who were not freed on the death of their master would serve for seven years only in the heir's household after which they would be considered free.

The immediate effect of the edict resulted in the release of thousands of men and women from unpaid domestic service. Unfortunately, there was practically no alternative employment into which the former slaves could be absorbed. They were jobless in a country where the cash incentive did not exist. Most came to some sort of terms with their former masters, many of whom were glad to be free of the traditional social responsibility to which slaves were entitled. But the remainder, destitute of support or employment, drifted into the towns to swell the ranks of the unemployed. Ethiopia became acutely aware that progress came with a whole new set of problems.

In 1924 Haile Selassie made a historic tour to the Near East and Europe. He sailed from Djibuti in April with an entourage including Ras Hailu and Ras Seyoum Mengesha, thirty servants, six lions, and four zebras. The tour took them to Jerusalem, Cairo, Marseilles, Rome, Paris and London. In Rome he met Benito Mussolini, who made vague promises of financial aid; in Paris he talked to the French about free port facilities of Djibuti, and in London he received no promises from the British. Nevertheless, he was successful in repatriating the crown of former Emperor Theodros II that had been stolen by England's Lord Napier after the battle at Magdala in 1867.*

The primary purpose of Haile Selassie's tour was to observe conditions and inspect modern inventions in the so-called civilized countries. On his return he was applauded and received wide acclaim from the populace for retrieving Emperor Theodore's crown from the British.

But Haile Selassie was troubled. He had seen in Europe things of far more value than Theodore's crown. He had seen something of industrial capacity that bred military might. He had also heard influential individuals condemning the backwardness of Ethiopia while speaking with envy of the country's wide open spaces as a potential new Eldorado. Haile Selassie felt that as long as Ethiopia lacked unity and the wherewithal to defend herself against an attack by an aggressor equipped with modern weapons of war, his country remained at risk for foreign intervention.

His problem was that dealing with such a threat meant that money that might be spent on schools or hospitals would have to be spent on armaments. The process of stabilizing the internal situation would be slowed.

"We need European progress only because we are surrounded by it," declared Haile Selassie before a European visitor to Addis Ababa. "That is at once a benefit and a misfortune. It will expedite our development, but we are afraid of being swamped by it." In Ethiopia, the opposition from the governors and church to change was overwhelming. The

**See the reference in Henry M. Stanley's book, The Abyssinian Expedition: Land Upon the Beach of Zoula. Sampson, Low and Marsted, Publishers, Publishers. London: 1896.*

anti-modernization climate existing in Ethiopia began in the 1860s during the reign of Theodore the Great when the country first confronted the modern West. During the ensuing decades, Ethiopia was able to resist alien domination, which many in the church believed was attributed to the fact that Ethiopia was a Christian nation, and had been so for centuries prior the age of discovery by the Europeans. The European method of conquering alien nations under the pretext of converting pagans to Christianity through missionary pursuits held little validity with Ethiopians.

Thus in the 1920s the Ethiopian traditionalists clung to its policy of isolation and aloofness from the West, even though political unity had not been firmly established within its borders, while externally the age of kings and Emperors had disintegrated and fallen. They were being replaced by a new political order of democratic, communistic and fascist institutions from abroad.

In December 1926, the pillar of traditional thought in Ethiopia, Abuna Matteos, died at the age of 83. The death of this religious leader signaled the end of an era of opposition to change because the *Abuna* (bishop in the Ethiopian church) represented a figure over whom Ethiopian Emperors exercised no control. Only the Council of Nicaea had the right of appointing a new *Abuna.* With this power vacuum the future Haile Selassie seized the opportunity to increase the powers of the *Echege* (head of the Ethiopian church) in all administrative church matters. The *Echege* was by tradition the counterbalance to the foreign-born *Abuna* who was invariably an Egyptian Coptic.

In October 1928, Teferi was crowned *Negus* (king) by the Echege in a silken tent in the Church of the Trinity, and Teferi Makonnen became the only Negus in the Empire. The Ethiopian Orthodox Church became independent from the Egyptian Orthodox Church and appointed its own patriarch. The second Ras Teferi Makonnen became the Negus (king). The result of this was that church was humbled, and Empress Zauditu was reduced to a figurehead.

On April 2, 1930, Empress Zauditu died suddenly at the palace in Addis Ababa, and the next day Negus Teferi was proclaimed Negus Negusti (King of Kings) and Lion of Judah under the throne name of Haile Selassie. Forty days of formal mourning followed the death of Queen Zauditu, who died during the rainy season when roads became quagmires and travel to the capital at Addis Ababa was impossible.

During the years of changes in Ethiopia, my father Adefris and my mother, Likelesh, were involved in domestic pursuits. The life of a kegnazmach involved many moves to

Negus (King)
Teferi Makonnen
(Haile Selassie)

administer different localities. In 1924 they moved to Kaffa, where their first son, Mekuria, was born. The next year they were transferred to Balé Goba, where their second son, Shengnew, was born and in 1929 they moved to Kulo Conta where their first daughter, Almaze was born. In 1930 when Haile Selassie was proclaimed Emperor, Likelesh and Adefris had three children. I was born thirteen years later, in 1943.

My father, Adefris, was 29 years old in November 1930 when Haile Selassie was crowned Emperor, and Mennen was crowned the Empress of Ethiopia. The new leader had witnessed or read about many changes in the country during the previous nine years. In 1928, a twenty-year "Treaty of Friendship" had been signed with Italy and a modernization program was beginning to make progress within the country. In 1929 a Belgian military mission was engaged to train the Imperial Guard from which the nucleus of a new regular army would be formed. No national army in the accepted sense had previously existed. Haile Selassie projected a standing army of about forty thousand men, trained along European lines under the direction of the Belgian military mission by officers imported from Europe.

Besides the creation of a standing army, Haile Selassie championed radical changes in education because he felt that an efficient administrative machine demanded educated men, and Ethiopia had very few men with a Western education. He felt that Ethiopia's future as an up-to-date nation depended on the progressives of a new generation since there was little to hope for from the traditionalists.

In Ethiopia at the time there existed no structure of state schools, colleges, and other academic institutions. The church had a virtual monopoly on education and encouraged the best pupils to enter the priesthood. The church also felt that universal education would undermine its authority, and its clergy were rigidly opposed to the spread of knowledge.

A few new schools had been opened in 1930 but the number was limited by the lack of teachers. Prior to becoming Emperor, Haile Selassie had proposed sending young men with special talents abroad but this was openly opposed by the Church, which objected to any foreign educational system that might convert Ethiopians into European religious beliefs not accepted as Christian by Ethiopians. The church in Ethiopia opposed both Protestantism and Catholicism. At public meetings held by the Ethiopian hierarchy, Adefris often heard Fetewrary Habte Giorgis compare the love of the Ethiopians to the love of a mother donkey. The

The Ethioipian parliament was established by His Majesty Emperor Haile Selassie for the first time in the long history ofthe country The building was completed after the Emperor had achieved significant economic and political progress for Ethiopia..

donkey, the Fetewrary observed, is the only creature that will sacrifice its life to protect its offspring.

The comparison did not register with Haile Selassie, who continued to pursue what he thought was right in the education of Ethiopian youngsters. His hard line on education was resented by the Ethiopian hierarchy as well as the majority of Ethiopians, who were unaware of the benefits of modern education and generally despised the idea of modern education. Haile Selassie sent a few young men abroad to study at his own expense. When they returned, only a few of the more enlightened Ethiopians were favorably impressed by this display of largess. Most disapproved.

Seven months elapsed from the time Haile Selassie was proclaimed Emperor and his coronation on November 2. During this time the capital city was prepared for the coronation. All Addis Ababa was refurbished, the police were given new uniforms, the main road to the *Gibbi* (palace) was resurfaced, new hotels were built to house visitors and the host of journalists who flocked in to report the celebration from around the world, and arrangements were made for distinguished guests to be brought by special train from Djibuti to Addis Ababa.

Addis Ababa, the "New Flower," was revitalized during these seven months, and the 10,000 foot Mount Entoto and other mountains surrounding it seemed to smile down at the transformation. On November 2, 1930, invited guests and peasants swelled the city to witness or to be near the historic event. A human tapestry of peasants, merchants, hillmen with spears, men-at-arms, women on foot, nobles on stallions with squires at their stirrups, ladies muffled on mules, Levantines, Armenians, Greeks, Syrians, Yemenese, Englishmen, Frenchmen, Spaniards, Italians, Americans, Japanese, Chinese, Africans, Arabians—all were there on that historic day to witness the coronation of the new Emperor and Empress.

Emperor Haile Selassie, King of Kings and the Lion of Judah, quickly accomplished what he had hoped for. The entire world became conscious of Ethiopia as an ancient and independent kingdom.

Adefris, his wife Likelesh, and their children—Mekuria, Shengnew and Almaze—were among the visitors to the capital. An atmosphere of expectancy, particularly among the young, filled the city. The deeds of the new Emperor had already been widely publicized prior to his coronation. He had built a hospital, sponsored a printing press for the publication of educational works, constructed a

African Hall, Addis Ababa, an Ethiopian gift to the United Nations. Emperor Haile Selassie was the sole broker in winning international acclaim for the Economic Commission for Africa.

college, brought electric lights to towns, imported a flour mill and woodworking machinery, built pipe lines to supply the town with water, and sponsored the construction of a large cotton plant consisting of forty-two machines to deal with all phases of cotton manufacture.

Whenever the slight figure of Haile Selassie rode through town, a hundred officers, chiefs, and white-clad rifleman ran beside and behind him. Not to be hindered, the crowds of the town would surge around them. Many times citizens determined to lay some plea before the regent would stop him. He always responded with good humor. The citizens regarded Haile Selassie as their own. He belonged to them. He was their prince, their brother, their man.

After the coronation of Emperor Haile Selassie, his modernization schemes accelerated. The Emperor established public schools and made an imperial proclamation that all parents who refused to send their children to school would be imprisoned. He negotiated with the National Bank of Egypt to purchase its subsidiary, the Bank of Abyssinia. He initiated a Sudanese-sponsored American engineering survey of the beautiful Lake Tana. He negotiated an arms traffic act with Britain, France and Italy that regularized the import of arms and ammunition for the new army. In 1931 he established the first Ethiopian constitution with a parliament representing a form of constitutional government. He introduced into the judiciary system a number of codified laws covering loans, bankruptcy, partnership, and limited liability companies.

The new emperor was determined to modernize and industrialize Ethiopia as quickly as possible. It was as if he was haunted by visions of pending disaster if he failed to do so. Having struggled for years with the traditionalists, he now felt liberated as the emperor to pursue a course for change.

Emperor Haile Selassie was first of all an Ethiopian attuned to the wants, desires and frailties of all his people from all classes. He felt that all knowledge was good as long as it was used constructively for the benefit of people. He was a teacher of the people who wanted to teach them the value of industry and understanding the problems of the present and the need to change. At the same time he was tolerant to the traditionalist who represented the unyielding past.

Above all, the emperor seemed to feel that time was running out for the independence of the kingdom. His goal was the unification of the country along with growth, development and security for the creation of a new and modern Ethiopia.

Ras Teferi and part of the family, 1928.

9

WAR IN EUROPE DIMS ETHIOPIA'S BRIGHT FUTURE

Dreams of a bright future for Ethiopia were dimmed by the ominous shadows of war looming heavily over the country early in 1933. Western powers were struggling through a period of economic depression while in the East the Bolshevik regime had fully established communism. On the European continent a new political system called fascism had entered the scene in Italy and Germany. The Italian, Benito Mussolini, had been a fascist dictator since 1925, and in 1933 Adolf Hitler became the Chancellor of the German Reich. The governments these leaders represented were militaristic systems in which the dictators held complete power, forcibly suppressed opposition, and criticized and regimented industry and commerce. Both Hitler and Mussolini were racist in their beliefs and fostered the theory of the superiority of their countrymen over all mankind.

Benito Mussolini's explosive public speeches were particularly disturbing to Ethiopians. Sample quotes: "Treaties are not eternal, and they are not unalterable; they are the chapters of history, not its epilogue." "Our policy will not be one of Imperialism which seeks the impossible." "I am obsessed by this wild desire which consumes my whole being. I want to make a mark on my era with my will—like a lion with its claw." "It is necessary to prepare for war, not tomorrow, but today." "We are hungry for land; we are hungry because we are prolific." "It is Italy's mission to civilize Africa. Her position in the Mediterranean gave her the right and imposed this duty upon her."

To Ethiopians the phrase, "to civilize Africa," was particularly ominous. For the past five centuries Europeans had used this goal as justification to capture, annihilate and subjugate native populations all over the planet. More importantly, the statements from Mussolini's speeches hit close to home. Italy was already on Ethiopia's northern border in the province called Eritrea and occupied an extensive area on Ethiopia's eastern border in a region called Italian Somaliland. In 1933 Ethiopia was the only country on the huge African continent that had not been "civilized" by European imperialism. It became patently clear to Ethiopians that Italy was planning an attack to conquer their land.

In addition to Mussolini's popularity, Ethiopians closely observed the rise of Adolph Hitler and the Nazi party in Germany in the 1930s. In the previous decade, while Hitler was in prison in 1923 for the crime of fomenting a Nazi revolution, he had written a book called *Mein Kampf* (My Struggle) in which he stated his vision for Germany's future, including his plan to conquer much of Europe. He sought revenge for Germany's defeat in the European World War I in 1918 and the resulting Treaty of Versailles, which confiscated German colonies.

In *Mein Kampf*, Hitler promised that all of the territories and colonies Germany had lost in the war would be retaken. Like Benito Mussolini, who proclaimed that Italy was "hungry for land," Adolph Hitler felt that the growing German nation not only needed but would also seize *lebensraum* (living space) for its people. Parts of Austria, Czechoslovakia, Russia and other lands to the east would be seized and added to the fatherland. Like Benito Mussolini, who stated, "It is necessary to prepare for war," Hitler breathed the threat of war by saying, "Conquest is not only a right, but a duty."

Thus in the 1930s four domineering forms of government emerged on the world scene—all of European origin, and all threatening the security and peace of mankind. In the East it was communism; in the West it was the political philosophies of democracy, imperialism and fascism. The countries involved promoting these government structures were Russia, the United States, Great Britain, Germany, and Italy.

All of these ideologies were beyond belief to the traditionalists in Ethiopia whose culture, based on a monarchical system of government, had survived for three thousand years. Keenly aware of the threat that colonial ambitions posed to his country, Emperor Haile Selassie worked feverishly to build a standing army capable of defending its territory. He recruited military personnel from Belgium and Sweden to assist him in building an army using modern weaponry. He chose Belgium and Sweden over countries much closer to Ethiopia because he did not want to face demands by neighboring countries for him to relinquish part of Ethiopia in exchange for the assistance.

In December of 1934 the first pretext for war occurred in the Walwal area of the Ogaden region in southeast Ethiopia. At Walwal can be found over a thousand wells, with the largest concentration of water in the arid Ogaden region. Each well was owned by a group of families, each group of wells by either the Rer Ibraham or the Mijurtin clans. Members of the Rer Ibraham clan came from Ethiopia or from British Somaliland, while members of the Mijurtin clan came from the Sultanate that had been annexed by Italy to form Italian Somaliland.

The dispute centered around which country owned the Ogaden, a territory extending 180 kilometers into Ethiopia from the Somali-Ethiopian border: Britain, Italy or Ethiopia. Historically, Ethiopia had ruled over this region as an integral part of her territory. For many years nomadic Somalis as well others in Ethiopia, had used this region for grazing their herds after bartering with land owners. Now Italy and Britain were contending for ownership and control of the Ogaden as part of their expanding colonial empires.

On the morning of November 23, 1933, Colonel Clifford and a delegation of British and Ethiopian commissioners arrived at Walwal. They found the wells occupied by about two hundred bands under the direction of a native Somali officer. Fetewrary Shifferaw pitched his camp to the north and stationed his Ethiopian troops across a line running roughly through the middle of the wells.

Military men accompanying the British Colonel pitched their tents in adjoining camps a few hundred yards away, and the Colonel raised the Union Jack (the flag of Great Britain). That night, the Italian frontier officer, Captain Cimmaruta, arrived at Walwal with a retinue of four hundred regular soldiers. Clifford asked the Italian officer to pull his men back. Cimmaruta refused and suggested that in order to avoid clashes, the two sides should mark out a provisional boundary line between the Italian and Ethiopian/British forces by scoring trees with knives. The Ethiopians feared this action would be tantamount to admitting that the Italians had a right to be so far inland. They refused to cooperate, pointing out that Cimmaruta had invaded the land by crossing the Somali-Ethiopian border and intruding well over 180 kilometers inside Ethiopia.

The afternoon of the day the foreign troops crossed the border and set up camp 180 kilometers into Ethiopian territory, November 23, two Italian military planes flew over the opposing camps. Twelve days later, on December 5, three planes and two light tanks appeared, and fighting broke out. By nightfall, 107 Ethiopians had been killed and forty wounded. Among the wounded was Fetewrary (General) Alemayu Goshu.

Four days later Blattengueta Herouy, Ethiopia's Foreign Minister, cabled the League of Nations to protest this assault on Ethiopian territory and to demand that the arbitration clause of the 1928 Treaty of Friendship be put in effect. On December 11 the Italian *charge d'affairs* responded with three counter demands:

1. That Dejaz Gabremariam, the chief of staff for the Ethiopian army, should come to Walwal in person and formally present his apologies to the representative of the Italian government while the Ethiopian detachment would salute the Italian flag;
2. That those responsible for the attack should be arrested and demoted, and then should also salute the Italian flag and be punished;
3. That the Ethiopian Government should hand over a Somali outlaw and the Italian subject Omar Smanthar, who the document claimed, was already guilty of the crime of the murder of the Italian Captain Carolei in the battle at Ogaden.

Emperor Haile Selassie took the courageous and wise step of appealing to the League of Nations regarding the encroachment of Somali-Italian forces into Ethiopian territory and to request a peaceful settlement. In doing this, the Ethiopian government stirred up trouble all over Europe. Debates at Geneva, open diplomatic warfare, and above all, anti-Ethiopian publicity, raged from one end of Europe to the other. Besides the military conflict inside Ethiopia's borders, other issues included in Ethiopia's appeal covered the actual issue of Walwal, the interpretation of grazing rights, the question of whether the frontier of Somalia was measured in nautical miles or statute miles from the sea, the fulfillment of the 1928 Treaty of Friendship, and responsibility for the deaths of Ethiopian soldiers on December 5. The appeal declared that the situation was an open crisis, in which Italy appeared to be a bullying aggressor. Politically it was a wise move by Haile Selassie because it brought the plight of Ethiopia to the attention of world leaders.

From the incident at Walwal events moved inexorably to war. There were two absolute rulers facing off for the confrontation: Mussolini in Rome, and Emperor Haile Selassie in Addis Ababa, each making diplomatic moves and counter moves to strengthen their prestige.

10

THE END OF THREE THOUSAND YEARS OF PEACE AND FREEDOM FOR ETHIOPIA

The Walwal incident provoked by the Italians in the Ogaden in 1934 marked a major turning point in the three thousand years of Ethiopia's history. Throughout the centuries the country had maintained its territorial integrity by resisting foreign invaders. It had also preserved its cultural heritage in the face of constant criticisms from foreign countries with a modern heritage of less than three hundred years.

The world in December 1934 was divided into the political spheres of capitalism, fascism and communism. Ethiopia and Japan were the only two modern countries ruled by emperors, and both countries were vulnerable to the pressures of the modern world to adopt their political systems and become a partner in their spheres of influence.

As an incident of confrontation between European powers over their colonial interests, the Walwal incident was also a prelude to the worst war in the history of mankind—World War II. The issues raised at Walwal were replayed repeatedly during the war in Europe.

The Italians, who had come last in the three-hundred year race for colonial expansion by European powers, believed that Ethiopia, the only uncolonized country in Africa, should become a colony of a new Roman Empire.

The beginning of the decline of the Ethiopian Empire started at Walwal.

Emperor Haile Selassie appealed to the League of Nations for intervention in what he considered to be a major crisis for his country. The appeal was justified by the fact that Ethiopia was a bona fide member of the League of Nations since joining it in 1923. Both Italy and Ethiopia had agreed to abide by the twenty-six Articles of the League's Covenant.

Specifically, Emperor Haile Selassie cited Article 10, which provided that "in any case of aggression against the territorial integrity and existing political independence of any member of the League, or any threat of such aggression, the Council shall advise upon the means by which the obligation of the members of the League to defend the victim of such aggression shall be fulfilled."

For months, the highest council of the 26-nation league vacillated. Benito Mussolini and his Italian followers interpreted the timidity of the council in condemning their actions as silent approval of the Walwal incident and justification to prepare for war to conquer the land.

Emperor Haile Selassie's presentiments of a pending war with Italy—even before Walwal—had already led to improvements of the Ethiopian army. The Belgians assisted him in building three battalions, three machine gun companies, two batteries, and a squadron mounted on heavy-duty horses imported from Australia. The fledgling Ethiopian air force at Janhoy Meda had twelve planes.

Haile Selassie solicited Swedish military advisers for assistance in January 1934 to launch an officers' cadet school at Holetta. The school was established in January of 1935 and was inaugurated by the Emperor in mid-April. It began with

120 cadets chosen from French-speaking pupils of the Teferi Makonnen and Menelek schools. The cadets ranged in age from 16 to 20. In the school there were 45 infantry cadets, plus 25 each for the engineers, the cavalry and the artillery.

The emperor sought help wherever he could find it. As the crisis grew in the early months of 1935, every train from Djibuti disgorged its quota of adventurers, journalists, and mercenaries. Arms and munitions poured into the country. Mercenaries came from Germany, Russia, Turkey, Egypt, and the United States to participate in warfare.

The Italian-Ethiopian War began in earnest during the early hours of October 3, 1935, when 100,000 Italian troops crossed the Ethiopian frontier from Eritrea. To an excited crowd filling Piazza Venezia in Italy, Mussolini announced: "We have been patient for forty years. Now we, too, want our place in the sun." Four days later the border towns of Adowa, Enticcio, and Adigrat were occupied without incident. Invading forces crossed the Mareb desert, and the planes of La Disperata took off and dropped their bombs. At Adowa, the Italian General hoisted the Italian flag. The Italians rejoiced in the belief that they had avenged their defeat by the Ethiopians in 1898.

By mid-October the Ethiopian counter attack had begun under the direction of military men who proved to be outstanding leaders in Ethiopian history. Under the leadership of Ras Mulugueta were 70,000 men; in Gondar, Ras Kassa had raised 160,000 men; on the left, Ras Imru moving from Debra Markos, had 25,000 men; Dejaz Ayalew Birru had raised 10,000 mountaineers from the Walkait and Semen.

For eight months Ethiopia was engulfed in violent warfare. In December 1935, Italian forces bombed Dessie. Emperor Haile Selassie joined the battle and began machine gunning the raiders. News of the Emperor's personal involvement in the military spread throughout the land and inspired the army as they desperately fought the enemy against armaments that were overwhelmingly superior to their own.

At the outbreak of the Italian invasion, my father, Adefris, who was on assignment in Kaffa, and Kenazmach Gezhagne Gobeze, a military officer, had been called to Addis Ababa by His Majesty Haile Selassie. The Emperor requested that they immediately go to the battleground in Machio Province in Northern Ethiopia to assemble a fighting force under Dejazemach Megensha Yilma, a cousin of the Emperor.

Adefris and Gehagne quickly assembled a cadre of warriors, mounted horses, mules, and donkeys and proceeded to the front lines of battle. As they traveled among the villages, *turmbas* (trumpets), drums and church bells sounded out to assemble the population. At these meetings the people were alerted that the country had been invaded by the Italians. All warriors were instructed to prepare to join the battle.

The Ethiopian forces assembled at Amba Alagi, the city known as the gate to central Ethiopia, to fight their first counterattack against the invading army. A total of 15,000 warriors from Beghemer Province were joined by 25,000 men from Gojjam Province along with 30,000 warriors from Wollo and other provinces, to clash with the Italians.

The battle began in the valley of the Takazze in western Tigre, a region held by the Italians, on December 15, 1935. After an all-night march the Ethiopian army forded the Takazee at two places, crossed the river, wiped out the Italian post and pressed rapidly up the mountain trail leading to the main Italian position. Bitter hand-to-hand fighting followed. The Italians were surrounded. Most of the Italian officers had been killed, and their tanks had become useless. Totally confused, the Italian army rushed downhill, only to be overrun by the Ethiopian army. The lorries the retreating soldiers threw themselves into were overturned and burnt. Ethiopian warriors leaped on tanks and killed crew members inside while fellow soldiers were overturning and burning other tanks. The disorganized Italian army was chased by two columns of Ethiopian soldiers at spear length up the road that led to the town of Enda Selassie. The Ethiopian forces were victorious, but only momentarily.

From Enda Selassie, thirty kilometers from Axum (one of the earliest centers of Ethiopian civilization), Ethiopian troops pursued the retreating Italian army. They utilized every means available. They rolled stones across paths where tanks were to travel. Italian drivers of the leading tanks were killed while others jammed into them from behind. The whole Italian column became a sitting target, and the Italian army retreated, setting up camp the following day within twelve kilometers of Axum.

This Takzee battle and Ethiopian victory proved that the Ethiopian army in open fighting with their swords and rifles were more than a match for Italian-trained troops even with their war tanks, which proved useless. In hand-to-hand fighting the Italian air force could not intervene and in such a battle, the Ethiopians were vastly superior.

But from the air it was the Italians who excelled. On December 23, 1935, Italian planes flew over the Ethiopian army and dropped not bombs, but cylinders, which broke as soon as they hit the ground, giving off a colorless liquid called mustard gas. When this liquid touched the exposed limbs of the Ethiopians, it burned the flesh. Many hands, feet and faces were scalded, and some of the soldiers were blinded. The effect on the Ethiopian army morale was terrifying. When Italian pilots flew over to drop their cylinders on Ethiopians in the Takzee valley, wounded and demoralized troops fell back. The first and best-led Ethiopian offensive was over, halted by the use of gas—mustard gas.

My father Adefris witnessed this atrocity. He saw children burned, mothers blinded, old people scalded. In all areas that the Italians subsequently became victorious, their victory was followed by burning houses, looting towns, poisoning rivers, killing domestic animals, murdering innocent people, raping women. Monks were assassinated, churches were destroyed. He was appalled at the wanton destruction of his countrymen.

For the next five months all Ethiopia was engulfed in warfare against the invading Italians. Towns throughout the land were shelled with cannons. Airplanes dropped bombs at random while town after town fell to the advancing Italians. By mid March northern Ethiopia was in Italian hands. The Ethiopian army disintegrated as the Italian troops moved out in all directions. April for the Ethiopians was a month of unrelieved disaster; for the Italians, a month of uninterrupted success. One after the other of the Ethiopian armies was defeated.

On April 1, 1935, Gondar, the historic capital of Beghemde, a province in northern Ethiopia and, until Emperor Theodore's reign, the imperial capital of Ethiopia, had fallen. The Italian flag fluttered in the early spring air over its buildings. The following day Emperor Haile Selassie ordered a retreat of Ethiopian forces. The retreating columns set off before dawn the next day, with the Emperor wearing a pith helmet and riding a white horse as he led the troops.

Italian planes dropped bombs and mustard gas on the retreating Ethiopian army. Out of 150 of the attacking planes only one was shot down, though 28 were damaged. All that day and the following day the pounding from the air continued. The rivers bled red with corpses. By the evening of the fourth day of April, the Emperor decided it was impossible to continue the retreat, and the columns turned and clambered back to Keren, a district in the Ethiopian province of Eritrea. There, in the comparative safety of the highlands, they dispersed, heading west in small groups across the country, moving only by night, all semblance of order or organization lost.

Emperor Haile Selassie vanished from the retreating group and went to Lalibela to pray. For three days he lost himself in a pilgrimage amongst the famous rock churches of Lalibela. After three days of prayer he headed southeast towards Dessie, the capital city of Wollo, only to find as he neared the town that it, together with the entire province of Wollo, had been abandoned. The Emperor and his escort went to the town of Fiche in Salale, the stronghold of Ras Kasa, on his way to Addis Ababa. Upon reaching Addis Ababa in May he found the city near panic, dreading the expected arrival of Italian troops.

Emperor Haile Selassie was still hoping for a miraculous solution from the League of Nations. He felt that the only way to stop the Italians was to bring pressure upon them from European powers. Out of the Ethiopian leader's desperation sprang the idea of making a direct and dramatic appeal to the League of Nations.

Haile Selassie knew that leaving Ethiopia to go to Europe at this time of trial would be viewed as cowardice by the Ethiopians. No emperor had ever fled from the Empire to appeal to foreigners abroad. Nevertheless, the emperor decided to make the journey. A train was made ready the night of Friday May 1, 1935. The Empress and the Imperial family boarded the train, bringing with them their household goods and many of the nobles and courtiers. The Emperor did not board the train in Addis Ababa because he knew the watchers in the city would surely have noticed him. Instead he and his immediate suite surreptitiously rode out of the city and joined the train at its second stop, 40 kilometers down the road at Debre Zeit, into exile.

On his arrival at Djibuti, Haile Selassie was received with military honors before embarking on the British cruiser HMS Enterprise that was to take him and his suite to Haifa, a city in Israel.

At Addis Ababa the Italian Army, headed by General Badoglio made its triumphant entry into the capital with 2,000 vehicles, including tanks and lorries, and 25,000 men. Eritreans marched by with flowers on their rifles, brandishing the swords they had captured from the Ethiopians.

As for the masses of the Ethiopian population, half-armed and disbanded warriors took to the hills as the Italians approached. One Ethiopian disguised himself as a monk by wearing a monk's cape. He said, "I watched the Italians marching into Addis Ababa on Tuesday and will begin killing them on Thursday. I will kill by night, and in the daytime, I will again become a monk." This was symptomatic of the mood of the population. Though the capital was occupied, the war, in fact, had just begun.

In Rome church bells rang, and loudspeakers summoned the populace to Piazza Venezia, where Il Duce, Benito Mussolini, appeared on the balcony and announced to the Blackshirts of the Revolution, "Men and women of Italy, Addis Ababa has fallen to the glorious troops of Marshall Badoglio." On May 9, 1936, again on the balcony of Piazza Venezia, to a wildly excited crowd, Mussolini proclaimed Vittorio Emmanuele III Emperor of Ethiopia. An imperial salute of 101 guns boomed out over the capital, and a mass chant echoed through the hordes of Italians assembled. *"Imperatore! Imperatore!"*

Ethiopia has witnessed the rise and fall of many great nations such as Babylon, Egypt, Greece, Ottoman, and Rome in its long and stoic existence. It has defied all attempts at its destruction as a nation. Although the fascist dictator, Mussolini, in his victory public address in Rome in 1935, arrogantly declared that Ethiopia was henceforth part of the Italian colonial empire, God did not take long to give His judgment. The blood of millions of defenseless Ethiopians murdered by Mussolini's army along with Ethiopia's prayer and unfailing trust in the justice of the omnipotent Creator was answered in time. Mussolini was killed by hanging in the streets of Rome by his own people.

In more recent history, Soviet imperialism schemed treacherous designs to divide the people of Ethiopia and killed millions more. And where is Soviet imperialism today?

Peace-loving Ethiopia today suffers at the hands of western super powers. Blueprints for colonial aggression were designed by the arrogant dictator Mussolini to force fragmentation and destruction of Ethiopian as a nation.

My advice to any super power that is trying to destroy Ethiopia is that it should think twice before launching such a malicious act, lest it bring on its own destruction. Today we ignore the signs in our world that are sent from God such as earthquakes, hurricanes, floods and wars throughout the world reminiscent of the last days of the great Roman power.

Whether the present ongoing attempts to destroy Ethiopia are by design or by lack of foresight on the part of foreign policy advisers in the United States such as Herman Cohen, the former Undersecretary of State for African Affairs and Paul Henze, a former CIA agent in Ethiopia, the mistakes are being carried out. It is time to take corrective actions and promote peace and a fair democratic system in Ethiopia and the rest of Africa.

Western powers, especially the United States, should recognize the sovereignty and territorial integrity of a historically united Ethiopia. It was a grave mistake for Western governments to undermine these principles. This trend culminated in the infamous London Conference of May 1991, organized by Herman Cohen, who was the U.S. Undersecretary of State for African Affairs.

In that conference the disintegration of Ethiopia was witnessed, signed and sealed. This action resulted in the secession of Eritrea and the installation of tribal-based government. The tribalization of Ethiopia came directly from plans for Ethiopia drawn by Mussolini in the 1930s.

Just as the Italians learned the hard way in the late 1890s and again in 1930, Ethiopians have a strong and historically ingrained sense of nationhood and independence. They have always fought to the death to defend their land. The present generation of Ethiopians is no exception.

I consider it my duty as a citizen of my adopted country, the United States, to say to all Americans that we must recognize the dangers of misguided policies. Most people in this country are uninformed about the underlying issues of the Ethiopian situation, and as a result will be taken by surprise when events lead this country to a quagmire of the sort we saw in Vietnam.

We stand on the Word of God stating that Ethiopia shall soon stretch her hands unto God (Psalms 68:31).

Genesis 2:10 to 2:13. "And a river went out of Eden to water the garden; and from thence it was parted, and became into four heads; the name of the first is Pison: that is it which compasseth the whole land of Havilah, . . . and the name of the second river is Gihon, the same is that which compasseth the whole land of Ethiopia; and the name of the third river is Kidekel, that is it which goes toward the east of Assyria; and the fourth river is Euphrates."

Psalms 68:31. "Ethiopia shall soon stretch out her hands unto God."

Acts 8:27-40. "And he (Philip) rose and went: and, behold, a man of Ethiopia, an eunuch of a great authority under Candace, queen of Ethiopians who had the charge of all her treasure, and had come to Jerusalem to worship, was returning and sitting in his chariot, read Esaias the prophet. Then the Spirit said unto Philip, "Go near, and join thyself to this chariot.' And Philip ran thither to him, and heard him read the prophet Esaias. . . ."

11

MY FATHER ADEFRIS

Even though the arrogant Italians were confident that they would prevail over the poorly geared and equipped Ethiopian soldiers, the Ethiopians for their part were determined to protect their nation and fought bravely.

The Italians came in hundreds of thousands with tanks and war machines and ammunition to kill the peace-loving Ethiopians. Tanks and bombs could not stop the determination of the Ethiopian defenders to stay a free people or weaken their commitment to fight for their freedom with their lives. When the Italians opened the front to fight, among the first Ethiopians to jump on top of the advancing Italian tanks was a young patriot by the name of Adefris Gebrie. In the tradition of his forefathers he fought in hand-to-hand combat with his sword. He jumped on top of moving tanks, pulled the operator out of the tank and killed him.

All the Ethiopians followed Adefris and did the same thing. The Italians, unprepared for the ferocity of combat and unrelenting attack by the Ethiopians became alarmed. Furthermore, they could not get effective air cover because the Ethiopians mixed with the Italians, making an air attack impossible without a disaster on the Italian side.

Because of the bravery he showed in the opening battle at Maichew, Adefris's peers gave him the following nickname:

Adefrisew Gebre
Yetoru Gebere

Translation: "Hero of the Battle" He kept this nickname throughout his life.

At the start of the war the Italians were defeated temporarily and retreated. Their next step was to come up with more power. In land fighting, victory was unthinkable against the Ethiopians. They had to use weapons available to them, such as spreading poison gas from the war planes.

This spread terror among Ethiopian fighters. It was an unspeakable situation. Thousands of burned bodies littered the battlefield—handless, footless, headless, eyeless bodies fallen everywhere.

Ethiopians were defeated in Maichew, overcome by technological advances in destructive warfare by a Western power. It took Ethiopians by surprise that a Christian power would rise up against Christians in Maichew, for the first time in the nation's history. The war ended in Maichew where it began, in Tede Mariam, the site of the St. Mary's church, 82 kilometers from Addis Ababa in the Lume District of the Shoa Province.

All remaining Ethiopians returned along with the emperor. Adefris was asked by His Majesty to follow him into exile, but Adefris replied, "All family, property, country and our people are in this country. We cannot leave for these savage unchristian pagans. We will fight to the last. Your Majesty should go and find political solutions." Adefris remained behind.

It did not take Adefris long to go to Lume (Kunche Medhanie Alem) to communicate with dispersed patriots to find new strategies to win freedom. The first person he contacted was Tulu Jada of Abichu (later Dezamatch Tulu Jada). The second person was Kegnazmach Bekele Gesitie, and the third was Kegnazmach Endaylaulu Wossnie. These four men began strategizing ways to defeat the invading Italians.

One strategy was to go to Addis Ababa through Bishoftu or Cheffe Donsa and kill as many Italians as they could, whatever the consequences might be. By then they had learned that Italians were bringing thousands of soldiers from Italy via Djibouti to reinforce their power.

Adefris came up with the idea that they should go to Tede Mariam instead of Addis to disrupt the railroad. They argued on this matter for a day. "Can we damage the railroad bridge to derail the train carrying the reinforcement troops and kill as many of the Italian soldiers as possible?" That was their goal.

Finally they agreed that they should take the trip from Kunche to Tede Mariam by way of Karra Michael. It took them one day to get there. They ruled against using a horse and walked in order to avoid being noticed by the enemy. They started to dig the railroad bridge in the night, hiding during the day in the shade of the trees in the forest. It took them several days to accomplish their plan.

One late Sunday afternoon, the train with more than 480 Italian soldiers aboard was derailed. All the soldiers and the train crew perished with no survivors. It was a disastrous day for the Italian invaders and a victorious one for Ethiopian patriots.

Italians did not attempt revenge because they thought it was an accident.

Adefris envisioned another plan to energize the struggle. He targeted the Golocha Belgian coffee plantation about 500 kilometers southeast of Addis Ababa. Adefris shared his idea with his colleagues, but it was not popular with them because of the distance and lack of communication. He could not persuade them to carry out his plan.

Tula Jada suggested that they do the things they knew how to do well. "Let Adefris go to Gololcha," he said, "and the rest of us will stay here and sabotage the Italians in many different ways." They agreed, and Adefris left for Gololcha via Wonji.

Wonji was known for its malaria problem at that time, but Adefris felt he had no choice. As Adefris was approaching Wonji, a horseback rider saw Adefris and stopped in the semi-desert area to talk with him.

This was unusual.

Adefris started to explain to the rider about the enemy, but the stranger did not show any concern. Adefris overpowered the man, took the horse and rode it to Serie (in Arusi). The horse died when he reached Keleta, a small bridge connecting Tera and Serie. Adefris continued on foot toward Serie where he went to a friend's house with bad news.

He told Woizero Beliyu Habte, the wife of Kegnazmach Bogalle of Serie and her son Taffess Bogalle, of the death of Keganzmach, who was killed in battle. After two days of rest, Adefris was given a horse and continued his journey to Gololcha. Within two days he arrived at Haro Giorgis, a church his father founded. He met his former servant who, unbeknownst to Adefris, had been appointed by the Italians as an informant. The servant walked the ten kilometers to Gololcha and informed the Italian representative that Adefris, the one who had fought the war at Maichew, had come back home.

Fortunately for Adefris, the interpreter happened to be Zewdie Farris, who was originally from Wollo, the birthplace of Adefris's father, Fetewrary Gebrie Aba Jirrie. The Italian representative assigned three soldiers to bring Adefris to the Italian court at Gololcha, but Zewdie told the Italian there were more important matters to do that day and that he would get Adefris the next day. The Italian agreed. Zewdie went secretly to Adefris and told him that three soldiers would be coming the next day to get him.

"Lie in bed and tell the soldiers you have diarrhea," he said. "Cough and pretend to be seriously sick." As a policy, the Italians did not want anybody in their compound with a communicable disease.

Adefris did as he was advised, and the soldiers went back and reported the situation to their commanding officer. A week and a half later Adefris went voluntarily to the Italian quarters. The Italian official said, "Have you been in Maichew?"

"Yes, sir," Adefris answered.

"What was your title?"

"I am Kegnazmach."

"Does that mean you were one of the leaders in the war?"

"Yes, sir."

"Who were the greatest fighters, Italians or Ethiopians?"

Adefris paused. "Will you allow me to ask you a question?" he said.

"Yes," the Italian said.

"Do you want to hear the truth or do you want me to tell you what you would like to hear?"

"Tell me the truth."

"If we Ethiopians had one tenth of your air power, Italians could not even step on Ethiopia's soil. I am telling you this because you were in the war, and you have seen the difference between us and yourself. Unfortunately, we lacked your modern war machines."

"Bravo, Adefris! Bravo, Adefris! You are a very honest man! Would you like to serve us now?"

"Yes, sir," said Adefris.

"In what capacity would you like to serve us?"

"I am a soldier."

"Would you like to be the chief of guard?"

Above: portrait of my father beneath the silver-plated sword he used in battles at Maichew and Ogadan. Below: The inscription in Amaharic is part of a memorial to my father in Nazareth. It tells the story of the Ogaden and Maichew battles.

"Yes, sir."

The Italian sent him to the ammunition warehouse to choose a gun for himself. When he got inside the store he noticed that all the guns in the store had been confiscated from Ethiopians. Adefris went back to the Italian chief.

"These were the guns we fought with in Maichew," he said, "and we lost the war. I would rather use spears or sticks."

"Bravo!" said the Italian. "You are very good."

He opened another store of newly arrived automatic machine guns. He gave Adefris a guard and let him pick his own staff to work with. Adefris familiarized himself with the people and the surroundings and within six months he was communicating with his old patriot friends, including Basha Mahalu from the Minnie area, Abebe Dagne and Teshome Wolde Emmanuel from Bulga, Shiferaw Wendye and Ahmed Abdul Kadir from Gololcha area. These patriots and their followers met secretly in Worego to plan attacks on the Italian invaders.

Friday mornings all the Italians gathered for breakfast. Usually a small aircraft brought information to them in the morning. At that time Adefris and his group walked into the breakfast hall and announced that all Italians were under arrest. They captured the Italians and imprisoned them. They raised the Ethiopian flag and burned the Italian flag that day and, a couple of hours later, executed the Italians.

Once again the coffee plantation, the largest in Ethiopia, was the property of Ethiopians. There would be no attempt after this battle in 1939 to regain control of Gololcha, Minni, Bekeksa, Chollie, Chulul and Guna.

In 1941 when the emperor returned from exile, Adefris came to see him from Gololcha, bringing with him a large number of horses and war machines. The emperor thanked him and several days later assigned Adefris as the administrator of the province of Gamu Gofa Kegnazmach. Adefris declined, after expressing his resentment of the emperor's appointment of other people to better positions after they had lived in exile during the years of the Italian occupation and escaped the struggle.

The emperor was offended by this criticism and sent Adefris to prison. But Prince Makonnen, Like Mequas Taddess Negash and Lij Assefa Nigatu intervened and pled for the emperor's forgiveness. The sentence of imprisonment was modified to house arrest. Adefris was sent to Nazareth where he lived like an ordinary Ethiopian to the day of his death.

The emperor offered him the title of Dejazmach in his absence through Grazmach Sahalu Defaye, but Adefris declined this position as well as personal invitations to see the emperor.

When he died in 1971 his death was broadcast over national radio in Ethiopia. He was buried with full honors with the old-style Ethiopian national guard giving full military honors. The silver-plated sword and spear he used in hand-to-hand combat against the Italians at Maichew and, before that at the Ogaden war, were confiscated from my house by the Dergue (a military strong-arm group) in 1975.

The sole purpose of my account of my father's life, accomplishments and death is to record the historical facts I inherited from my father. My admiration of His Majesty Emperor Haile Selassie for his great accomplishments, sacrifices and leadership for Ethiopia is unaffected by the differences in later years between the emperor and my father.

ጃንሆይ

ባኅረሱ ተነከሱ

ከአሰፋ አደፍርስ

ጃንሆይ

ባጎረሱ ዕጃቸውን ተነከሡ

ከአሰፋ አደፍርስ

ዋሺንግተን ዲሲ

መስከረም ፲፱፻፺ ዓ. ም.

ልዩ ምሥጋና

ይህን መጽሐፍ ሳዘጋጅ ከጎኔ ሳትለይ ያበረታታችኝን ባለቤቴን ወ/ሮ አምሳለ ኃይሉን እንዲሁም በጉልበትና በገንዘብ የረዱኝን ልጆቼን
ቴዎድሮስ አሰፋን
መቅደላዊት አሰፋን
አደፍርስ አሰፋንና
ዒዛና አሰፋን አመሠግናለሁ።
በተለይም የመጨረሻው ልጃችን ወጣት ዒዛና ከፍቶኝ ስተክዝ በሳቅና በጨዋታ ስለሚያስደስተኝ አደንቀዋለሁ።

በመጨረሻም የዚህን ሥነ ጽሑፍ ውበትና ጌጥ በማስማመር የረዱኝን አቶ ለይኩን ብርሃኑንና በኃሳብ ያልተለዩኝን ዶ/ር ይልማ ጉልትነህን ከልብ አመሠግናለሁ።

አሰፋ አደፍርስ

መታሠቢያነቱ

ካለማወቅ ወደ ማወቅ ጉዞዬን ለጀመርሁበትና የዕውቀት ብርሃን ላየሁበት ለናዝሬቱ ዓፄ ገላውዴዎስ ት/ቤት እንዲሆን አበርክቻለሁ።

አሰፋ አደፍርስ

ማውጫ

መግቢያ

ይችን መጽሐፍ ለማዘጋጀት ካነሳሱኝ ምክንያቶች ከብዙ በጥቂቱ የቀዳማዊ ኃይለ ሥላሴ ኢትዮጵያን ለማልማትና ዘመናዊ ለማድረግ ያደረጉት ጥረት ሁሉ በዚህ ትውልድ ዘንድ ትቢያ ለብሶ መታለፉን በማየቴና በመፀፀቴ ነው። ግርማዊ ቀዳማዊ ኃይለ ሥላሴ ከማንም ጋር መወዳደር ቀርቶ እርሳቸው ባረፉበት ቤት ውስጥ ሊጠለሉ የማይገባቸው ፀረ ሕዝብ ፀረ አገር በሳቸው ላይ የሚወረውሩት ሐሰት የሚናገሩት ጸያፍ ከካንሰር በሽታ የባሰ ደዌ ነው። « በማን ላይ ቆመሽ እግዜርን ታሚያለሽ።» እንደሚባለው እርሳቸው ባቋቋሙት ት/ቤት ተምረው ዛሬ ባጎረሱ ዕጃቸውን ተነከሱ ሆነ። ይህ ትውልድ ለጃንሆይ ወይን ተክለው እንዶድ ያፈራ ዛፍ ሆኗል። ነገር ግን የሚያጽናናው ሥራቸው ሕያው ነው። ታሪክ ክብሩንና አድናቆቱን አይነፍጋቸውም። እሳቸውም ከአሁን ወዲያ የሚያደንቃቸውም ሆነ የሚነቅፉቸው ታሪክ ብቻ ነው። ስለሆነም «ብር ላበደረ ጠጠር» እንዲሉ በግል ጥረታቸውና ትጋታቸው ኢትዮጵያን ከአሥረኛው ወደ ሃያኛው ክፍለ ዘመን ያደረሱ ስለሆኑ ይህን መሳይ አመለካከትና አገላለጽ ያቀረቡላቸው የሠጧቸው ጸሐፊዎች ጥቂቶች አይደሉም። የኢትዮጵያ ሕዝብ ጃንሆይን በማጣቱ የቀረበትንና የተቀማውን በየትም አካባቢ በማንኛውም የኢትዮጵያ ቋንቋዎች የሚናገረውን የምንሰማው ነው።

አሁንም ሳላወሳው የማላልፈው ጉዳይ የዘመናችን ምሁራን ለዚህ ዕድገትና ዕውቀት ያደረሷቸውን ንጉሠ ነገሥት በጠላትነት መመደባቸውን ነው። የእርሳቸውንም ክብርና ስም ዝቅ ያደረግን መስሏቸው ምንም ከማያውቁት ወታደሮች «ሂድና ቁም» ትዕዛዝ እየተቀበሉ የጎሊናቸውን ወቀሳ ፍላጻ ታግሠውና ችለው ሥራቸውን እንዳልሆነ ሲያደርጉት መመልከቱ

ለአገር ልማት ለሕዝብ ደኅንነትና ዕድገት ለጣሩና ለደከሙ ኢትዮጵያውያንና ኢትዮጵያውያት ጀግኖች ውለታና ክብር የማንሠጥና የማናውቅ ከሆነ ይች አገርና ይህ ትውልድ እንደሚበን አደራና እንደሚተን ጢስ በከንቱ መቅረታቸው ነው። ይህን የመሰለውን ሁሉ የማየት የማስተዋል አደራ ከእያንዳንዳችን ዘንድ ፍፁም ይጠበቃል። የዜግነትና የሰብአዊነትም ግዴታ ይሆናል ብዬ አምናለሁ።

ኢትዮጵያ የሦስት ሺህ ዓመት ነፃነት ያላት አገር ናት ሲባል እንደ ቀላል ነገር ያለበለዚያም ልማዳዊ አባባል አድርገን የምንመለከተው ጥቂቶች አይደለንም። የእነዚህን ዘመናት ሂደት ውጣና ውረድ ምን ያህል ረጅምና ብዙ መሆኑን የምንለካው ኢትዮጵ ያ ከደርግ መዳፍ ከወደቀችበት ቀን ጀምሮ የደረሰውን ጭንቀትና መከራ ላይ ያተኮርን እንደሁ ነው። ይህን ካልሁ ዘንድ እንዲታይ የምጠቁመው ከሐረር እስከ አዲስ አበባ ያንድ ወር ጉዞ ይፈጅ የነበረውን በዓርባ አምስት ደቂቃዎች እንዲደረስ ያደረጉ የሠራቸውን ውጤት በዓይናቸው የተመለከቱ ቀዳማዊ ኃይለ ሥላሴ መሆናቸውን ነው።

በዘመነ ደርግ የዓፄ ቴዎድሮስ የዓፄ ዮሐንስና የዓፄ ምኒልክ ዘመን ታሪክ ሲጻፍ ቀዳማዊ ኃይለ ሥላሴ ላይ ሲደርሱ የብዕር በትኋቸውን ልጓም የያዙ ያለበለዚያም የቮልስዋገን መኪናቸውን ፍሬን ተንጠራርተው የረገጡና ያቆሙ ጸሐፊዎች ምንኛ የኅሊና ጸጸት ይይዛቸው? ከአንተነት ወደ አንቱነት ካለማወቅ ወደ ማወቅ የደረሱበትንና ያለፉበንትን የሕይወት ጎዳና ማፍረስ ራስን ለጥቅም መሸጥ ያለበለዚያም ራስን እንደ መግደል የሚቆጠር የታሪክ ወንጀል ነው።

በዓለም መድረክ ኢትዮጵያ የነበራትን ክብር ከደርግ ማግሥት የት ናት? ማን ነን? ምሥክርነቱንና ትዝብቱን ለዚህ ትውልድ ተመራምሮ እንዲደርስበት እተወዋለሁ። ያገርን ባህል ሳናውቅ ሳንጠነቅቅ የሰው

ወርቅ እያደምቅ የሚለውን ሳናቢተውል የደረስንበትንና
ያለንበትንም አሁንም ለተመልካች መተዉን
እመርጣለሁ ግን የቀዳማዊ ኃይለ ሥላሴን ጥረት
ድካምና የወገን ፍቅር ቦታ ሳንሰጥ ባሳየነው ኢባሕላዊ
ጠባይ በለፈለፉ ይጠፉ ሆነናል። ለዚህምኮ ነው ክብር
በሰው ዕጅ ሲያዩት ያምር ሲይዙት ይደናገር
እንደሚባለው ሆኗል።

ቢነገር ቢነገር ወደማይሠለቸው ወደ ቀዳማዊ
ኃይለ ሥላሴ የትምህርትን ማስፋፋት ኢትዮጵያውያንን
ማሠልጠን ወዳደረጉት ጥረት ለጥቂት ጊዜ
ልመልሳችሁ። ጃንሆይ ዘመናዊ ትምህርትን ሲያስፋፉ
የመኳንንቱ የባላባቱ የሃይማኖት መሪዎች ተቃውሞ
ጥቂት አልነበረም። ይህ ነው የማይሉት ታላቅ ተጋድሎ
አድርገዋል። ከሚደርሱት ተቃውሞዎችም ውስጥ ጎላ
ያሉትን ብናይ እንገረማለን። እነሱም የሚከተሉት
ነበሩ።

ልጆቻችን ይህን ዘመናዊ ትምህርት ከተማሩ
ሃይማኖታቸውን ይለውጣሉ። ለአገራቸው ባዳ ይሆናሉ።
የወገንና የአገር ፍቅር ያጣሉ። የሚሉ ፍርሃቶች ነበሩ።
ጃንሆይም እኒህን ሥጋቶች የሚሸረው መልሳቸው
በወላጅና በልጅ መካከል ያለውን የፍቅር ሠንሰለት
ከፍተኛነት በመመልከት ባጠገባቸው ለተሰበሰቡት
መኳንንት እንዲህ የሚል ምሳሌ ነገሯቸው።

አንድ ፈላስፋ ከሰው ዘርና ከእንስሳት ልጁን
ከራሱ አብልጦ የሚወድ የቱ እንደሆነ ለማወቅ ፈለገ።
ከእያንዳንዱም አገርና እንስሳት አቅርቦ ልጆቻቸውን
በሚነድ እሳት ጉድጓድ ውስጥ እንዲጣሉ ሲያደርግ
ወላጆች ቀርበው እንዲመለከቷቸውም አደረገ። ይህ
ሲሆን የልጆቻችንን መቃጠል አናይም ብለው ሲሸሹ
ከሰው ኢትዮጵያዊ ከእንስሳት ጎሽ ልጆቻቸው
ከተጣሉበት የእሳት ጉድጓድ አብረው ገቡ ይባላል።
በማለት አስረዷቸው።

ይሁንና ጃንሆይ ትምህርት የዕድገትና የሥልጣኔ ምንጭ መሆኑን የተገነዘቡት ገና በልጅነታቸው ከአባታቸው ከልዑል ራስ መኮንን ጋር ለንደንን በጎበኙበት ጊዜ እንደሆነ ይናገራል። ስለዚህም ትምህርትን ለማስፋፋት ሲሉ የትምህርት ሚኒስትርነቱን ቦታ የያዙት ራሳቸው ነበሩ። በዚያን ጊዜ ነው ይባላል አንድ ካናዳዊ አማካሪያቸው በተለይም የአዲስ አበባ ዩኒቨርሲቲ ኮሌጅ በሚከፈትበት ጊዜ ይህን የማንንም የተራ ሰው ልጅ ከፍተኛ ትምህርት ከሠጡት ውሎ አድሮ የሥርዓቱ አፍራሽና አጥፊ ነው የሚሆነውና ለከፍተኛ ትምህርት የሚገቡት በጥናትና በጥንቃቄ ይሁን ብሎ ስለነገራቸው በመቆጣት በዓርባ ስምንት ሰዓት ከኢትዮጵያ እንዲወጣ አድርገውታል ይባላል።

ግርማዊ ቀዳማዊ ኃይለ ሥላሴ በሕዝባቸው ዕኩልነት ለትምህርት ከፍተኛ ጥረት ያደረጉ ታላቅ መሪ ነበሩ። ኢትዮጵያውያን ሁሉ ልናከብራቸውና ልናደንቃቸው ይገባል። ለዚህ ትውልድ ባለአደራውና ባለውለታውም ናቸው። በዚህ አጋጣሚም ለማቅረብ የምሻው የዚህ መጽሐፍ ሺያጭ በከፊል በስማቸው ኢትዮጵያ ውስጥ ለሚቋቋመው የቀዳማዊ ኃይለ ሥላሴ በጎ አድራጎት ድርጅት መርጃ እንዲሆን በባለቤቴ በወ/ሮ አምሳለ ኃይሉና በልጆቼ በቴዎድሮስ በመቅደላዊት በአደፍርስና በዊዛና አሰፋ አደፍርስ ስም ሳበረክት በታላቅ ደስታ ነው።

ማን ያርዳ የቀበር

ማን ይንገር የነበር

አገራችን ኢትዮጵያ በታሪክ በቋንቋ በሥነ ጥበብ በማኅበራዊ ኑሮ በዕጅ የሚዳሰሱት በዓይን የሚመለከቱት ገሀዳዊ የሆነ የሦስት ሺህ ዓመት ታሪክ በእያንዳንዱ ዜጋ አዕምሮ ተቀርጾና ተስሎ ለመገኘቱ ምሥክር አያሻውም። ይሁንና እንደ ሥልጣኔያችን ጥልቀትና ምጥቀት እንደ አጀማመራችን ሂደት የት በደረስን ነበር? ይህ በእያንዳንዳችን ኅሊና ውስጥ ያለና የሚኖር የጸጸት ግርዶሽ ነው። ይሁን እንጂ ባሕሉን ወጉን ልምዱን የጠበቀ ታሪኩን ሃይማኖቱን ያከበረ ምን ይሉኛልን ከባህሉ አዛምዶ የያዘ ሕዝብ አብሮ መኖሩ የታወቀ ነው። እንዴት ቢሉ አንተ ትብስ አንቺ ትብሽ ተባብሎ መኖር ያውቃልና ነው። ይኼውም በተለምዶ ከራሱ ሌላውን ያስቀድማልና ነው።

የሰው ልጅ በመዋዕለ ሕይወቱ ሁለት ነገሮች አብረውት ይጓዛሉ። እነሱም ማጣትና ማግኘት ናቸው። የእነዚሁ ዘርፎች ደግሞ ኃዘንና ደስታ ይሆናሉ። ይህም ይታወቅ ዘንድ በሥነ ፍጥረት ሕግ የሁለት ተቃራኒ ነገሮች አብሮ መገኘት ነው። እንግዲህ ሕይወት ይህን መስሎና አክሎ የሚታይ ነው።

የዚሁ መግለጫ ደግሞ ኑሮው ውጣ ውረዱ መራቡ መጠማቱ ሁሉ በአንድነት ሆኖ ነው። ስለሆነም የዚህ መንጸባረቂያ ሆነው በመታየት ላይ ያሉት ወገኖቻችን በሌላው ጎን ያገራችን ዕድገት የሚያስታውሱን አንድ አባባል አለ። እሱም «ፊተኞች ኋለኞች ይሆናሉ።» የሚለው ነው። በገነት በልምላሜ ውስጥ እየኖርን ከሰማይ የሚወርደው ዝናም ከመሬት ላይ ያለው ልምላሜና በውስጥ የሚገኘው ማዕድን ሞልቶ ተርፎል። ነገር ግን ወገኖቻችን ሰማይ ኮርኔሱ ድንጋይ ትራሱ ሆነው ይገኛሉ። በየአብያተ ክርስቲያናቱ ቅጽሮች በየመስገዱ ደረጃዎች

በየአደባባዩ መስኮች በየንግድ ቤቱ በራፎች ላይ እንደ ቅጠል ረግፈው እንደ አቧራው ተነስንሰው በየቦታው ወድቀው ተበትነዋል። ለዕለት ጉርስ ለዓመት ልብስ የሚሞሁትንና የሚያለቅሱትን ወገኖቻችንን ስንመለከት እጅግ ያስደነግጣል። ያጸጽታል። ስቅስቅ አድርጎም ያስለቅሳል።

ይህን የመከራ ጽዋ ለዚህ ትውልድ ዕጣ ፈንታ እንዲሆን ያደረግን ያስደረግን የተባበርን የገፋፋን ተመልክተን ዝም ያልን ሁሉ የጥትፋቱ ተጓዳኞች መሆናችንን በምፀት በአሽሙር በሽሙጥና ራስን በማመጻደቅ የማናመልጠው የጋራ ወንጀል መሆኑን ለትዛዜ ሳላቀርበው ማለፉ እጥፍ ድርብ ጥፋት ያደርገዋል።

ማነው ንፁሑ ማን ነው ከበደሉ ነፃ የሆነው? በኔ ግምት ሁሉም ወደሚለው እመርጣለሁ። እያንዳንዱ ደጁን ቢያፀዳ ሮም ትፀዳለች የተሰኘውን አበባል ልብ እንበል። ሕይወት የሚያጠፉ ነፍስ የሚቀጥፉ የመቅሠፍት መልእክተኞች ሲመጡ መንገድ ያሳየ ቆሞ ያነጋገረ ጥፋት ሲያደርሱ ከኛ አምባ አይደለም ብሎ ዝም ያለ ተራውን መጠበቁን ረስቷልና ተባባሪ ነው።

ከቀጣፊዎች ጋር የተባበረ የወገኑን ነፍስ ሸጦ በሰው ሕይወት ነግዶ መኖር መሆኑን ተገንዝበነው ይሆን? ጥቂት ገዳዮች ብዙኃኑ ሟች ሲሆን እንደሚታረዱ እንስሳት ራስን ማስቀጠር አይደለምን? ጥፋተኛን ያውም ገዳይን ስናይ ዝም ማለቱ አሁንም ከገዳዩ ያላነሰ ወንጀል ሠሪዎች መሆናችንን እንድናስብበት የምሬት የኃዘንና የጸጸት ማሳሰቢያዬ ነው።

በመግቢያዩ ላይ ያወሳኋቸው በረንዳ አዳሪዎች በቅጽረ ቤተ ክርስቲያን የወደቁት በየመንገዱ የሚለምኑት የአሁኖቹ የመንገድ ተዳዳሪዎች ሁሉ የዕለት ምግብ በማግኘታቸው ተመስገን ባዮች ሆነዋል። ሌሎቻችን በስደት በመንጠላወዝ የምንኖረውም ደስተኞች ሆነን ሳይሆን መስለን ከምናዝንበት

ከምንተከዝበት ቦታ ወጥተን ወደምንዘፍንበት ወደምንስቅበት ሠፈር እግሮቻችን ያለዚያም የምናሽከረክራቸው መኪናዎቻችን እንዲያደርሱን እናስገድዳቸዋለን።

እንግዲህ ይህን መሳይ ተግባር ስናደርግ በተጨባጭ ሁኔታ በወገኖቻችን ዘንድ የሚደርሰውን መከራ ሳናስብ ችላ ብለን ይሆን? ሕፃናት ልጆቻቸውን ትተው የተሠወሩ የታሠሩ የተገደሉትን ሁሉ በጥሞና እንዘክር። ስለ አገራቸው ፍቅር ስለ ወገኖቻቸው ክብር ሲሉ መከራና ግፍ የሚደርስባቸውና የሚቀበሉ አሉ። በዚህም የተነሣ ደፍረው በተናገሩ አሻፈረኝ ባሉ የገና ገናም ያሳድማሉ ሕዝብ ያነሳሳሉ ያምጻሉም እየተባሉ ይሠቃያሉ። ይህ ብቻም አይደል። ማን ቢወልድ ማን? በሚለው በሕዝባችን በወገናችን ላይ በወረደው የዘር ክፍፍል ወረርሽኝ የታሠሩ የታፈኑና የተገደሉም አሉ። ታዲያ የምንገኘው ከእንዲህ ዓይነቱ ዘመን ላይ ነው።

የራሳቸውን መቃብር ቆፍረው በሚቀበሩበት ዘመን ራሳችንን ስናታልል ይሁን እያረሩም መሳቅ በሚባለው ፈሊጥ ተወስደን እንደሆነ አይታወቅም በዝምታ ተሞልተን ዝም ጭጭ ብለናል። ይህን የመሠለም ተግባር ፈጽመናል። አገርን ወገንን ከዚህ ዓይነቱ መከራ ለማውጣት ከሚጮሁት ጮኸናል። ከሚያለቅሱት አልቅሰናል። እንዲያውም ለተወሰኑ ግለሰቦች ሥራ አድርገን ሳንተወው ተባብረናል። ግን ፕሬዚዴንት ጠቅላይ ሚኒስቴር ለመሆን ፍላጎት ያላቸው የሥልጣን ሱሰኞች በጎ ፈቃዳችንን ወደ ክህደት አዛውረውታል። ሁሉን ርግፍ አድርገን ትተንና ዘንግተን በእንዲህ ዓይነቱ ሁኔታ ላይ ላለን ሁሉ ወዮልን።

ሆነም ቀረ ሁላችንም ለአገራችን የምናበረክተው ማንኛውም ትንኟ ጉዳይ ሁሉ እንደ ዛፍ ዘር ናት። ታድጋለች። ትንኟን የዋርካ ፍሬን እንመልከት። ከትንኟ ትልቁ ይገኛልና! ትንኟ ስጦታችን ጋን በጠጠር እንደሚደገፍ ትረዳለች። ይህን ከመሰለው

ብሔራዊ ተግባርና ምኞት ተስፋ ተለይተን እንዲሁ እንደሚደበደብ ከበሮ ውስጠ መንፈሳችንን ባዶ እናድርገው። ያልሆነውን መስለን ያልሠራነውን ዋሽተን የሌለንን በልጽገን አንታይ። አንድ ወንበር አሥር ሰው አይቀመጥበትም። የተሠራው ላንድ ነውና! አንዲት ሴት ለአሥራ ሁለት ጎልማሶች ሚስት ልትሆን አይገባትም። አትችልምም። እንዲሁም በተፈጥሮ ጥንቸል ከአቅሟ በላይ ሆና እንደ አንበሳ ልትጮህ አትችልም።

በሌላ በኩልም አሜሪካ አገር የሚኖር ሁሉ አዋቂ መካኒክ ጠፈር ተጓዥ የዩኒቨርሲቲ ፕሮፌሰር አይደለም። ሊሆንም አይችልም። የሚሆኑትና ያሉትም በተግባር የሞከሩትና የተረጎሙት ብቻ ናቸው።! ይህን እንገንዘብ። ሁለት እግር ያለው ሁሉ ባንድ ጊዜ ሁለት ዛፍ ላይ ሊወጣ አይችልም። ይህም ተብሎና ተነግሮ ያደረውም ለዚሁ ነው።

ምኞት የተስፋ ልጅ ነው። ተስፋ ደግሞ የተግባር ንድፍ ነው። ተስፋ የሌለው ሕይወት ደግሞ መብራት የሌለው የጨለማ መንገድ ነው። በአገራችን የተለመደውን ማስታወሱን እናስበው። ሩቅ ሳንሄድ አባት ለልጁ የሚመኝለት እንደራሱ ሳይሆን አብልጥና ከፍ አድርጎ ነው። እንደ ምሳሌም የሚጠቀሰው አራሽ ልጁ በቦታው ተተክቶ ርስቱን ባድማውን አስጠብቆ እንዲኖርለት ተተኪ እንዲሆነው ነው። ነፍጠኛው ደግሞ የራሱን መሣሪያ የሚወርሰው ተኩሶ የማይስት ፈረስ የሚኮረኩር ዳር ድንበር የሚያስጠብቅ ጠላት የሚያሸብር ወገን የሚያስከብር እንዲሆንለት ነው።

እንግዲህ ይህ በእንዲህ እንዳለ ሥልጣኔ የምዕራቡ ዓለም ሥልጣኔ ነፋስ በኢትዮጵያ ላይ መንፈስ ጀመረ። ነፋስ ነውና መንፈስ ሽው ሽው ማለት ቀጠለ። እየቆየ ሲሄድ የነበረውን የቆየውን የኖረውን ባሕል ሞራል ቋንቋ መገልበጥ ጀመረ። በመጨረሻም ወደ ዓውሎ ነፋስነት ተለውጦ ጣራ ግድግዳ ኃብት ንብረት ማጥፋቱን ተያያዘው። በዚህን ጊዜ ነበር በኢትዮጵያ ቁራዎች መጮህ የጀመሩት። ቀበሮዎች መርባትና መራወጥ ቀጠሉ። አገር ሲጠፋ ምልክቱ ይህ

ነው። ታዲያ ሥልጣኔ ምነው በጃፓን አማረ? ምነው አፍሪቃ ሲሆን መልከ ጥፉ ሆነ? ፀባዩ ብልሹ ሥነ ምግባር የተለየው ምን አደረገው? እንደ ጃፓኖች የምንበላውን አብልተነው የምንጠጣውን አጠጥተነው የምንለብሰውን አልብሰነው የምንናገረውን አናግረነው ቢሆን ኖሮ እንደ ጎፉች በቅሎ አለት ላይ ፈጥፍጦን ባላረፈ ነበር። ይሁንና ሆነ።

ለሠራተኛ ዋጋው ይገበዋል

ያገራችን በሬዎች የሚስቧቸው ቀንበሮች የሚጎትቷቸው ሞፈሮችና ማረሻዎች የአምስት ሺህ የአመጣጥና የመኖር ታሪክ አላቸው። እንደ ትውልድ ሲወርድ ሲዋረድ እስካሁን በስፋት ሲገኙ የዓይነትም ሆነ የቅርጽ ለውጥ ሳያደርጉ እንደ ቤተ መዘክር ዕቃዎች በእያንዳንዱ ኢትዮጵያዊ ገበሬ ቤት በአገልግሎት ላይ ይገኛሉ። በአንጻሩ ግን ሰውን መድፈር ሃይማኖት መሻር በባዶ ሆድና ዕጅ መንቦጣረር ካገር ውስጥ ሞልተው ተርፈው ቀይ ባሕርንና ሕንድ ውቅያኖስን ሞልተውታል።

የኛ መሠልጠን የራሳችን የሆነውን ጥለን ባዶ ዕጅ እስከ መሆናችን ድረስ ሆኗል። ከዚህ የአመለካከት ጎዳና ተነሥተን ተጉዘን የት እንደ ደረስን ያለንበትን ሁኔታ ዘወር ያለዚያም አንገትን ዘቅዘቅ አድርጎ መመልከት ነው። ከዚህ ላይ ከደረስን ፊታችንን አዙረን ወደ አንድ የታሪክ ዘመን እንመለስና እንይ። ከየት ወዴት? የሚለውን ጥያቄ ይመልስልናል። ይህንም ኃሳብ ሳቀርብ በሕይወቴ ያለፍሁበትና የገጠመኝ መሆኑን በማረጋገጥ ነው። ይህንም ምሥክርነት የምሠጠው አቤቱታዬንም የማቀርበው ለተተኪው ትውልድ ነው። ይህ በከፍተኛ ደረጃ ግንዛቤ እንዲያገኝ በብርቱ እማፀናለሁ።

ያ በረጅምነቱ በውበቱ በሥነ ጽሁፉ በባሕሉ በሃይማኖቱ በቅርጻ ቅርጹ እጅግ ከኛ ይልቅ የዓለምን ጠቢባን ዓይን አውልቆ ለመውሰድ የሚስበው ኢትዮጵ

ያዊው ታሪካችንና ጥንታዊው ስልጣኔያችን ተጉዞ ተጉዞ እኔ ከተወለድሁበት ዘመንና ጊዜ ደርሷል።

እንግዲህ በኔ ሕይወት ያየሁትን ስመሠክር ለሠራተኛ ዋጋው ይገባዋል። የሚለውን የመጽሐፍ ቃል በማስታወስ ነው። የኔ መዋዕለ ሕይወት የሚጀምረው ከቀዳማዊ ኃይለ ሥላሴ ዘመነ መንግሥት ነው። እኔ የተወለድሁት ጠላት በጀግኖች ኢትዮጵያውያን እግሩን ተሠብሮ አንገቱን ተመትቶ በተባረረበት ብሔራዊ ስሜት እጅግ በጎለበተበት ዕድገት ፍቅር አንድነት በየአደባባዩ መለያና መታወቂያ ዓርማ ተደርጎ በተቆጠረበት ዘመን ነበር። ጠላትን አሸንፎ አገርን የራስ ያደረጉበት ዘመን የነፃነት የአርነት ዘመን ነውና መከራ ወጣ ተድላ ደስታ ጀግንነት መጣ። ተብሎ የሚነገርበት ጊዜ ነበር።

እኔ ምሥክርነቴን የምሠጠው ከልጅነት እስከ ዕውቀት ያለፍሁበትንና የታዘብሁትን ነው። ኢትዮጵያ ይህ ነው ተብሎ በአድናቆት የሚነገርላት ታሪክ ያላት አገር ናት። እንኳንም ኢትዮጵያዊ ሆንሁ ቀርቶ በሆንሁ ኖሮ! የተባለበት ጊዜ እንደነበር የትናንት ትዝታ ነው። ለማስረጃም ያህል በአገራችን ይኖሩ የነበሩት የግሪክ የአርመን የዓረብና የኢጣሊያን ሰዎች ለኢትዮጵያ ዜግነት ደጅ ይጠኑ እንደነበር የትናንት ትዝታ እንደነበር የውጭ ጉዳይ መዛግብቶቻችንን መመልከቱ ጉዳዩን በቂ ያደርገዋል።

ይህም ሊሆንበት የቻለው ምክንያት ይህም ትውልድ ሊኮራ የሚገባው ብቸኛ የነፃነት ዓርማ ሆና በአፍሪቃ ምድር እንደ ፀሐይ ታብራ የነበረችውና ጠላቷን ድባቅ መታ የመለሰች ብቸኛ አፍሪቃዊት አገር በመሆኗ ነው። በዕጅ የያዙት ወርቅ ከመዳብ ዕኩል ነው። ተብሎ የሚነገረው ምሳሌ ከዚህ ላይ መጥቀስ እውነትነቱን ይኩለዋል። ያሳምረዋል። ያረጋግጠዋልም። ያለዚያም ያጎለዋል።

ኢትዮጵያ በዚህ ጣዕሟ በዚህ መዓዛዋ በዚህ ለዛዋ ጊዜ ለተወለደና ላደገ ትውልድ ኩራቱና ክብሩ ወኔው እስከ እንቁርቱ ድረስ ነው። ይህን ሁኔታ ለዚህ

ትውልድ ሳይናዘዙ ሳይመሠክሩ ማለፉ አባት ለልጁ የቀበረውን ወይንም ያከማቸውን ኃብት ንብረት ለልጁ ሳያወርስ በሜዳ በትኖት እንደ መቅረት ይቆጠራል። ስለሆነም ከአቅሜና ከችሎታዬ በላይ ነው ብዬ የማላስበውን በውስጤ እንደ ተዳፈነ እሳት ዘወትር ውስጥ ውስጤን የሚያቃጥለኝን ያገር ክብር ፍቅርና ነፃነት ሳልናገር እናዳላልፍ ኅሊናዬ እጅግ አድርጎ ያስገድደኛል። ለዚህም ነው በኃይል በወኔ የምወተውተው።

እንግዲህ ይህ ሲሆን የዓይን ምሥክርነቴን የምገለፀው በሚከተለው አኳኋን ነው። ከሰባት ዓመት ዕድሜዬ ጀምሮ ያየሁትና የማውቀው እንዲህ ባንድ ጊዜ ፈትቶ የሚያፈሱት አይደለም። ይልቁንስ እየቆነጠሩ ያሊያም እየዘገኑ የሚያድሉት እንጂ! እንዲያው ላቀራረብ እንዲያመች ቃኝተነው የምናልፈው ጉዳይ ሁላችንም የምንኮራበቱ የዓፄ ምኒልክ ዘመነ መንግሥት ነው። የዓፄ ምኒልክ ስም ሲጠራ በቅድሚያ በበላይነት የሚያንፀባርቀው ታላቁ የዓድዋ ድል የኢትዮጵያውያን ጀግንነትና አንድነት ነው።

በዚህ ዘመን ነበር ራስ መኰንን ወልደ ሚካኤል የዳግማዊ ዓፄ ምኒልክ መልእክተኛ በመሆን የኪንግ ጆርጅ በዐለ ንግሥ ላይ እንዲገኙ ወደ እንግሊዝ አገር የተላኩት። ያ ጉዞ ታሪካዊነት አለው። ማየት ማመን ነው። የሚሉት አውሮጳውያን ትክክለኛነትን በቂ ምሥክርነት መሆኑን ለማረጋገጥ ነው።

ይሁንና በዚያን ጊዜ ራስ መኰንን አብረዋቸውና ይዘዋቸው የሄዱት ልጃቸውን ልጅ ተፈሪ መኰንንን ነበር። በዚያን ጊዜ የልጅ ተፈሪ ዕድሜ ዘጠኝ ዓመት እንደ ነበር ይነገራል። ይሁንና ራስ መኰንን ከሄዱበት ጉዳይ የበለጠ ትኩረትና አድናቆት ያሳደረባቸው የእንግሊዞች ዕድገት ልማትና ሥልጣኔ ነበር። ይህንኑም ለልጃቸው አጥብቀው በአድናቆት ነግረዋቸውና አስረድተዋቸው ነበር ይባላል። እሱም አገራችን

ኢትዮጵያን እንዲህ እንደ እንግሊዝ ማድረግ ምንም የሚቸግር ነገር የለም። ለዚህ ሁሉ ጥበብ ዓይኑና ቁልፍ ትምህርት ብቻ ነው ብለዋቸው ነበር። የልጅ አእምሮ ነጭ ወረቀት ነው የተሠጠውን ይይዛል እውነት ነውና ልጅ ተፈሪ መኰንን ያባታቸውን ምኞትና ምክር እንደ ልብስ ተጎናጽፈውት እንደ ማግ አጥልቀውት እንደ ቀሩ ይነገራል።

ያም አባባልና ምክር በኀሊናቸው ተሥሎ ለመቅረቱ ጃንሆይ በትምህርት የነበራቸውን ዕምነት ታላቅነትና ኢትዮጵያን ወደ ዘመናዊ ሥልጣኔ ለመምራት ያደረጉት ጉዞ ዋና ዋቢ ነው። ያን የልጅ ተፈሪን ጉብኝት እንደ መልካም ዘር በቅሎና አድጎ ፍሬ መሥጠቱን ያስመሠከረው በዘመነ መንግሥታቸው ያከናወኗቸው ታላላቅ ሥራዎቻቸው እንደ ሆኑ ከአሁኑ ይያዝልኝ።

ቀዳማዊ ኃይለ ሥላሴ ገና አልጋ ወራሽና ባለ ሙሉ ሥልጣን በነበሩበት ጊዜ ት/ቤቶችን ማሠራት ወጣቶችን ወደ አውሮጳ በመላክ በትምህርት ላይ የነበራቸውን ጽኑ ፍላጎትና ዕምነት በተግባር ሊተረጉሙት መነሳታቸውን ነበር ያረጋገጡት። በአፈ ታሪክ ወላጆቻችን ሲያወሩት የሰማነው ጃንሆይ በአልጋ ወራሺነታቸው አንድ ሺህ ወጣቶች መልምለው ወደ ውጭ አገር ለትምህርት እንዲሄዱ ለንግሥት ዘውዲቱ ያቀርባሉ። ንግሥትም የወጣቶችን ብዛት ተመልክተው ይህን ሁሉ እንዴት እንልካለን? ለእናቶቻቸውም እዘኑላቸው ብለው ሦስት መቶው ብቻ እንዲሄዱ ፈቀዱ ይባላል።

የዘመናዊ የትምህርት ሂደት

ጃንሆይ ንጉሠ ነገሥት ከሆኑም በኋላ ትምህርት የአውሮጳን ሥልጣኔ ማርኮና ነጥቆ የሚያመጣ ኃይል እንደሆነ ተገንዝበውታል። ስለዚህም ዘመናዊ ትምህርት ወደ ኢትዮጵያ እንዲገባ ቦታውን አመቻቹለት።

በመጀመሪያ ለሕዝቡ አርዓያ ይሆናሉ ብለው በማሰብ ለጊዜው ሊታዘዟቸው የሚችሉትን የትምህርት ጥቅም ይገባቸዋል የሚባሉትን የሹማምንቶችንና የባላባቶችን ልጆቻቸውን ወደ ት/ቤት እንዲልኩ ያስገድዷቸዋል።

ይህም ሲሆን ሞግዚት ተቀጥሮላቸው በአዳሪ ትምህርት ቤት በመክፈት ነው። ራሳቸውም በቅርብ እየጎበኟቸውና እያጽናኗቸው ነበር። ይህን ወደፊት እንመጣበታለን። ይህን ኃሳብ ማለት ልጆቻቸውን ወደ ት/ቤት በመላክ የተባበሯቸው ጥቂቶች ነበሩ። ምክንያቱም ብዙና የተለያዩ የጠላት ቅስቀሳዎች በአገረ ገዥዎችም ዘንድ ሆነ በወላጆችም ዘንድ ተጽእኖ አሳድሮ ነበር። ይኼውም አስኳላ ት/ቤት ልጅን መላክ ሃይማኖቱን ይክዳል። ከሥነ ምግባር ውጭ ይሆናል። የሚሉ ነበሩና ነው። ምናልባት ትንቢት ነበር ብለን እንቁጠረው? በዚህ ኃሳብ ከተጨነቁት አገረ ገዥዎች መካከል አንዱ የቤት አሽከራቸውን ለግዳጅ ሲሉ በልጃቸው ምትክ እንደላኩና እንዳስተማሩ ይነገራል።

የትምህርት ጉዳይ በቀላሉ የሚታይ ነገር አልሆነም። ልጁን ትምህርት ያላከ ሰው ካህናቱ እንዲገዝቱ መንግሥት ዓዋጅ በማውጣት ልጁን ያላስተማረ እንደሚቀጣ ሁሉ ተደነገገ። በዚህ ሁኔታ ዘመናዊ ትምህርት ላይ ርብርቦሽ መደረግ ቀጠለ።

ይህ በእንዲህ እያለ ነበር ያ ያሸመቀው የኢትዮጵያ ጠላት ለሁለተኛ ጊዜ የኢትዮጵያን ዕድገትና የሥልጣኔን ዕድገት ለመግታት ወረራ የጀመረው። ጃንሆይ ዓዋጅ ነግረው ወደማይጨው ዘመቱ። የጠላት ጦር እየለ። እየገፋም መጣ። ትግሬን ጎንደርን ያዘ። በዚያን ጊዜ ነበር የኢትዮጵያ መኳንንት ጃንሆይን ለዓለም መንግሥታት አቤቱታ ለማቅረብ እንዲሄዱ በመወሰን በግድ የስደት ጉዞ እንዲጀምሩ ያስደረጓቸው።

ጃንሆይ አውሮጳን ከረገጡበት ጊዜ ጀምሮ ስለ አገራቸውና ስለ ሕዝባቸው ሌት ከቀን ደፋ ቀና ይሉ ነበር። እንዲያውም ኢጣሊያኖች ጃንሆይን ብዙ ገንዘብ

ካገኙ አቤቱታቸውን አቋርጠው አርፈው አንዱ አውሮጳ አገር ቤት ገዝተው ኑሮ ይጀምራሉ በሚል ኃሳብ እጅግ መጠኑ የበዛ ገንዘብ እንስጥዎት አርፈው ይቀመጡ ብሎ ጠላት ፈተና አቅርቦባቸው ነበር። ነገር ግን አገሬንና ሕዝቤን በገንዘብ አለውጥም አሉ።

ከዚያም ግርማዊ ንጉሠ ነገሥት በብዙ ትግል ጀኔቫ ለዓለም መንግሥታት ተወካዮች አቤቱታቸውን አሰሙ። ያ የጃንሆይ ንግግር ትንቢት መሆኑ ያልገባቸው አፍጩባቸው። ተንጫጩባቸው። ብዙም ጊዜ አልፈጀ። መላ አውሮጳ በሁለተኛው ዓለም ጦርነት ተማገደ። በዚያን ጊዜ ነበር የጃንሆይ ንግግር ትንቢት መሆኑ ግንዛቤ ያገኘው። ጃንሆይ ያን የስደትና የአቤቱታ ዘመቻ ፈጽመው በድል አድራጊነት ወደ አገራቸው ሚያዚያ ፳፯ ቀን ፲፱፻፴፫ ዓ. ም. ተመለሱ።

የኢትዮጵያ አርበኞችም ጠላትን መግቢያና መውጫ አሳጥተው አሳደው በመውጋት የድሉ ባለቤትም ሆኑ። ጃንሆይ አውሮጳ ላይ ያደረጉት ንግግር ለዓለም ሕዝብ መወያያ ፈጠሩለት። ይኼው ንግግር ለአገር ውስጥ ጀግኖች ደግሞ ከፍተኛ የመንፈስ ማጎልመሻና አጋዥ ኃይል ነበር። እንዲሁም በተጨማሪ በአገር ውስጥ ያለው አርበኛ በየጊዜው ከግርማዊነታቸው ይደርሰው የነበረው ማበረታቻና ማነቃቂያ ደብዳቤ ራሱን የቻለ ሌላው የጦር መሣሪያ ነበር። ይህን እንደ ጋሻቸው አንግተው ሞራላቸውን አድሰው ለትግላቸው መርህ አድርገው የተጠቀሙበት ጀግኖቻችን ቁጥር ጥቂት አልነበረም። ይህን ከታላቅ ግንዛቤ ውስጥ ልናስገበው ይገባል።

ዘወትር ያለማቋረጥ የእግዚአብሔርን ስም ከአንደበታቸው የማይለዩት ንጉሠ ነገሥት ለአርበኛው ሁሉ በሚጽፉት ደብዳቤ ላይ የእግዚአብሔር ኃይል ከኛ ጋር ነው በርቱ። በድል አድራጊነት እንወጣለን። የሚለው ቃል የአርበኛው የስንቁ ማጣፈጫ የትጥቁ ማጥበቂያ ነበር። ጃንሆይ እንዳሉትም በአምስት ዓመት ከመከራ ዘመን በኋላ ድል በዕጅ ገባች። ሰላም በኢትዮጵያ ምድር ሠፈነች። ከጦርነት ወደ ልማት

ጉዞው ተጀመረ። ከዚህ በኋላ ያለውን ጊዜና ዘመን መጀመር ያበሠሩት አዲስ ዘመን በሚለው ንግግራቸው ነበር። ይህን ቃል እስከ ዛሬ ይዞት የሚገኘው ብሔራዊው ጋዜጣችን ነው። እሱም አዲስ ዘመን ጋዜጣ ነው።

ይህ አዲስ ዘመን ትኩረቱን ያደረገው በትምህርት ላይ ነበር። ጃንሆይ በትምህርት ሁሉን ነገር ማድረግ እንደሚቻል በጽኑ ያምኑ ነበር። ስለዚህም ለትምህርት የሠጡት ትኩረት እጅግ ከፍተኛ ደረጃ ነበር። ትምህርት የሥልጣኔ የበር ቁልፍ መሆኑን ከተገነዘቡት ዋል አደር ያለም ነበር። ስለዚህም ለብዙ ጊዜ የትምህርት ሚኒስትርነቱን ቦታ ራሳቸው ጃንሆይ ነበር የያዙት።

አዳሪ ት/ቤቶችን በማነጽ በማደራጀት ለተማሪዎች ልብስ መጽሐፍ ፍራፍሬ ሳይቀር በማደልና በማበረታታት ዘመናዊው ትምህርት በኢትዮጵያ ሥር እንዲሰድና ኢትዮጵያ በልጆቿ እንድትገለገል አድርገዋል። በጃንሆይ ያልተመሠረተ ያልተቋቋመ ምን አለ? አሁን የሚታየው ሁሉ ፋብሪካው የሙያ ማሠልጠኛው መገናኛው የየብሱ የባሕሩ የዓየሩ የባቡሩ የስልኩ ወዘተ... ሁሉ ተደማምሮ ነው። አሁን ግን የምናየው ያ የነበረው የጠፋበት ይባስ ብሎም የተዘጋበት የፈረሰበት ጊዜና ዘመን ነው። ጃንሆይ በሕዝቡ ዘንድ የነበራቸው አክብሮትና አድናቆት እጅግ ከፍተኛ ስለነበር በወቅቱ ሕዝቡ እንዲህ እያለ ያሞካሻቸው ነበር።

በኃይለ ሥላሴ ያልተማረ፤
ማዘኑ አይቀርም እያደረ።
ስሙ እንዲታወቅ በዓለም ሁሉ፤
ኃይለ ሥላሴን ጠቅል በሉ።
ኃይለ ሥላሴ አባታችን ያሠሩልን ቤት፤
የምንማርበት የጥበብ ሁሉ ዓይነት።
የምንመገበው ማርና ወተት።

ጃንሆይ በአዳማ

ለዚህ ትረካ ፍጻሜ ማስረጃ አድርጌ የማቀርበው የራሴን ሕይወት ምሥክርነት ነው። ይኼውም ኢትዮጵያ ከየት ወዴት? የሚለውን የሥልጣኔ የመሸሻል ጉዞ ያሳያል። በኔ ምሥክርነት የማቀርብላችሁ እውነታ ከጋማ ከብት ወደ ጄት ብላችሁ ርዕስ እንድትተሠጡት አደራዬ ነው። ብዙ ዘመንም ወደኋላ አልጎትታችሁም። እጅግ በጣም ከቅርቡ ነው የማስጀምራችሁ። ይህም ዘመን ፲፱፻፵፮ ዓ. ም. ነው።

በዚያን ጊዜ ግርማዊ ቀዳማዊ ኃይለ ሥላሴ ናዝሬትን ለመጎብኘት የመጡበት ዘመን ነበር። እኔም በዚያን ወቅት ንጉሠ ነገሥቱንና ንጉሣውያን ቤተ ሰቦችን ለመጀመሪያ ጊዜ በጆሮ የሰማሁትን በዓይኔ ያየሁበት ቀን ነበር። የማይረሳ ትዝታ አብሮኝ እስካሁን ያለ ነው። በዚያን ዘመን በአቶ ተስፋ ገብረ ሥላሴ ዘብሔረ ቡልጋ በሚዘጋጁት የመማሪያ ደብተሮች ላይ የጃንሆይ የግርማዊት የልዑል አልጋ ወራሽና የልዑል መኰንንን ፎቶግራፎችን በማየት ብቻ ነበር ምን እንደሚመስሉ የምናውቃቸው።

ጃንሆይ ከአዲስ አበባ ናዝሬት የመጡት በትንሽ አውሮፕላን ነበር። ከደብረ ዘይት በታች ገና የጥርጊያና የኮረኮንች መንገድ ነበርና ነው። ቀኑ ቅዳሜ ሰዓቱ ከጧቱ አምስት ገዳማ ይሆናል። ቦታው የቅዱስ ገብርኤል ቤተክርስቲያን የነበረው በወንጂ መንገድ ላይ ነበር። ጃንሆይ ሊመጡ ነው። የሚባለው ወሬ ከተማውን ንዶታል። ከዚያ አውሮፕላን ማረፊያ ሜዳ ከፍ ከፍ ያሉት የት/ቤት ልጆች በጨርቅ ወይንም በቡቱቱ ኳስ ይጫወታሉ። እኔም ከተመልካቾች አንዱ ነበርሁ።

ከጥቂት ጊዜ በኋላ ባላምበራስ ደምሴ የሚባሉ የማዘጋጃ ቤቱ የጭቃ ሹም መጥተው ሁላችንንም ከሜዳው አባረሩን። ወዲያው ራቅ ብለን ስንመለከት በአሮጌ አዳማ በኩል አውሮፕላን ብቅ አለች።

ለብዙዎቻችን ያ ቀን አውሮፕላን ቆሞ ማየቱ የመጀመሪያችን ጊዜ ነበር። ያለንን አድናቆት ጉጉት ገምቱት። ልባችን ስቅል ብሎ ነበር። ወዲያው አውሮፕላኗ አረፈች። እንደ መኪናም እየተሽከረከረች ከመንገዱ ስትደርስ ቆመች። በሯ ተከፈተና ጃንሆይና ዕቴጌ መነን ብቅ አሉ። እልልታውና ጭብጨባው ቅልጥ አለ። ቀጥሎም ልዑል አልጋ ወራሽ ልዑል መኰንን ልዑል ሣህለ ሥላሴ ልዕልት ተናኘ ወርቅ ራስ እምሩ ራስ መሥፍንና ሌሎች ሴቶችም ነበሩ። ከአውሮፕላኗ ወረዱ።

የሚገርመው ነገር ንጉሡ ነገሥቱን ተቀብሎ የሚወስድ መኪና አልነበረም። ነገር ግን ዶ/ር ዋንገር የተባሉ አሜሪካዊ ከኃይለ ማርያም ማሞ ሆስፒታል አንድ ቫን ይዘው መጡ። ጃንሆይና ዕቴጌ ልዑል አልጋ ወራሽ ልዑል መኰንን ሊዕልት ተናኘ ወርቅ ሆነው በዶ/ር ዋንገር ቫን በኋላ የወባ ማጥፊያ ድርጅት ወደ ሆነው ቤተ መንግሥት አመሩ። የቀሩት ደግሞ ራስ እምሩ ራስ መሥፍንና ሌሎቹ በአቶ አየለ ይግለጡ የንግድ ቫን ሆነው ወደ ቤተ መንግሥቱ ተከተሉ። ሁሉም ጉዟቸውን ወደዚያው አመሩ።

እኛ ግን ከልዑል ሣህለ ሥላሴ ጋር ጨዋታ ያዝን። ልጆች ነንና ፕሮቶኮል ምን እንደሆነ አናውቅም። ከበናቸው ስለነበር የት እንዳሉና እንደነበሩ ዓይታዩም ነበር። ሁሉም ሲሄዱ ተለይተው ቀሩ። የለበሱትን በመነካካት ጋሼ ይህ ምንድን ነው? ከሚለው ጥያቄ ጀምሮ የሳቅና የጨዋታ የውይይት አደባባይ ፈጠርን። በዚህ ሁኔታ ብዙ ጊዜ አሳለፍን።

በዚህ ሁኔታ እንዳለን ለካስ ልዑሉ ከቤተ መንግሥት ባለመገኘታቸው ሽብር ተፈጥሮ ነበር ይባላል። ወዲያው ጀኔራል ሙሉ ጌታ ቡሊ ከበደ ጉደታን አስከትለው በእግራቸው በችኮላ ከኛ ዘንድ ደረሱና ልዑል ሣህለ ሥላሴን በተማሪዎች መካከል ሆነው አገኟቸው። ወዲያውም ይዘዋቸው ሄዱ። ያች ቀን ከልዑል ሣህለ ሥላሴ ጋር ያወጋሁባት ምንጊዜም አትረሳኝ። የልዑሉም መልክና አነጋገር ሁሉ ከፊቴ

ነው። ይህን ትዝታና ሁኔታ ካስገነዘብኳችሁ ወደሚቀጥለው ጉዞ ልውሰዳችሁ።

የወቅቱ ትራንስፖርት

ከዚህ ላይ ላሳያችሁ የምፈልገው በዚያን ጊዜ የነበረውን የመንገድና የትራንስፖርት ሁኔታ ነው። ከናዝሬት ውልንጪት ለመድረስ በባቡር ወይንም በበቅሎ ነበር። ነገር ግን ላንድሮቨር የነበራቸው ሰዎች የሚወስድባቸው ጊዜ ከሦስት ሰዓት በላይ ነበር። ውሊንጪቲ ከናዝሬት አሥራ አምስት ኪሎ ሜትር ርቃ የምትገኝ የወረዳ ከተማ ናት። በዚያን ዘመን በናዝሬት ከተማ መኪና የነበራቸው ሰዎች ሁለት ብቻ ነበሩ። እነሱም ሚ/ር ባከ የዓፄ ገላውዴዎስ ት/ቤት ዲሬክተርና ሙሴ አልባንዲ የተባሉት የአርመኑ ተወላጅ ኢትዮጵያዊ በተለይም የሚታወቁት የኢትዮጵያን ሕዝብ መዝሙር በዘመናዊ ኖታ ወይንም ሙዚቃ ያቀነባበሩ በመሆናቸው ነው። የሁለቱም ሰዎች መኪናዎች ሂልማን የተባሉት የእንግሊዝ ሠራሾች ነበሩ። ኢትዮጵያ በእኔ ዕድሜ እንዴት እንደ ነበረች ግንዛቤ አግኝተናል።

ይሁንና ከአዲስ አበባ አሩሲ ከአዲስ አበባ ሲዳሞ ከአዲስ አበባ ከፋ የሕዝብ ትራንስፖርት የሚባል ነገር ፈጽሞ አይታወቅም ነበር። የዘመኑ መጓጓዣዎች የነበሩት ትሬንታ ኳትሮ እየተባሉ የሚታወቁት የጭነት መኪናዎች ነበሩ። ከዕቃው በላይ ሰው ተጭኖ በአቧራና በዝናም እየተለወሱ በየመንገዱ እያደሩና እየተጓዙ ነበር ከሳምንት በላይ ጊዜ ተወስዶ የሚደረሰው።

አንድ እኔ የማውቀውን ላውጋችሁ። ከሜኤሶ ዐሰበ ተፈሪ ከአሥራ ስድስት ጊዜ በላይ መኪናው በመንገዱ ጉራንጉርነት ይያዛል። በተለይም ዝናም በጣለ ቀን ያ እየተቆፈረ ሲወጣ ሲሄድ ሲቆፈር መኪና በሞተር ሳይሆን በግፊ ይሽከረከራል ማለቱ ሳይቀል

አይቀርም። ያገሬው ነጋዴ ያወጣለት ስም ያ ኩሬራ የተባለው የእንግሊዝ ፎርድ መኪና ይህን ሁሉ ውጣ ውረድና መከራ በማሳለፍ ነበር ከመኤሶ ዐሰበ ተፈሪ መንገደኛ ያመላልስ የነበረው። ይህም ብቻ አይደለም። ከሮቢ ናዝሬት ለመጓዝ ካንድ እስከ ሁለት ሳምንት ሲፈጅ አንዳንድ ጊዜ ደግሞ መኪናው በጪቃ ተይዞ ከወር በላይ የሚያሳልፍበትም ጊዜ ነበር።

ያ ሁሉ ቌንቅ በሾፌሮችም ሆነ በተሳፋሪዎች ላይ ይደርስ የነበረው በቀዳማዊ ኃይለ ሥላሴ ተወገደ። መንገድ ሥራ ተጀመረ። የሕዝብ ማመላለሻ አውቶቡስ ገባ። ይህ የትራንስፖርት ድርጅት ሳይስፋፋ እንደ ምሳሌ የሚጠቀሱት መኪና መግዛት ይታይ የነበረው የሀብታምነት የታላቅነት የክብር ምልክት ስለነበር ሰዎች እንዲሁ ይገዙ ነበር።

ይህም ይታወቅ ዘንድ በናዝሬት ከተማ መኪና የሚገዙና ያላቸው ሰዎች መታየት ጀመሩ። ከታወቁት ከሁለቱ ሰዎች ሌላ አቶ ታዬ ወንድማገኘሁ አቶ አብደላ ሐኪሜ የመጀመሪያው የምስማር ፋብሪካ በኢትዮጵያ የጀመሩ ፈራሪ የወ/ሮ ጥሩነሽ ባለቤትና አቶ ዘገዬ ብሩ የመኪና ባለቤቶች ሆኑ። እንዲሁም በሐረር በልበልቲ ከተማ የታወቁት ሀብታሙ ገበሬ አቶ ደሳለኝ ከልካይ ፕሪሞ ቲፓ የተባለች ላንድሮቨር በመግዛት የመጀመሪያ ሰው ናቸው።

መኪና መግዛት እንጂ መንዳትም ሆነ መጠገን ሌላው የማይታወቀው ተግባር ነው። ይሁንና መንዳቱንም ተምረው የሚያሽከረክሩም ብቅ ብቅ ማለት ጀመሩ። ይሁንና ከመንዳት በስተቀር ሌላ የሚታወቅ ስላልነበረ አንድ የሚያስቅ ጨዋታ ላቅርብላችሁ። አቶ ተስፋዬ ገብረ ሥላሴ የሚባሉ ጠበቃ አንዲት ቮልስዋገን መኪና ይገዛሉ። ከአሰላ ወደ ናዝሬት እየነዱ ይመጣሉ። ሞተሩ ይቀዝቅዝ ብለው ጥላ ካለበት መንገድ ያቆማሉ። የፊቱን ኮፈን ከዳን ቢከፍቱ ባዶ ሆኖ ያገኙታል። ወይኔ ጉድ ሆንሁ በማለት ይቆጫሉ። እሳቸው አቋርጠው የመጡትን መንገድ ተከትለው የደረሱባቸውን ሁሉ እያስቆሙ ሞተር ከመንገድ ወድቆ ዓያችሁ ወይ? በማለት በጥየቃ

ሲወተውቱ ከተጠያቂዎች ሰዎች አንዱ የትሬንታ ኳትሮ ባለቤት ኢጣሊያኒያዊው ሲኞር አርላንዶ ሞተሩ ያለ ከኋላው እንደሆነ ከፍቶ በማሳየት ከድንጋጤያቸው አዳናቸው እየተባለ የወቅቱ መሳቂያ ትዝታ ነበር።

ያ ሁሉ ትዝታ የልጅነት ነውና አብሮ ኗሪ ነው። ሲታወስም ይኖራል። እንግዲህ ከዚህ ዓይነቱ ሁኔታ ተነሥተን ዕድገታችንን በመቀጠል ወደ ውጪ የተላኩት ተምረው ተመለሱ። ከፍተኛ የትምህርት ተቋሞች ተሠሩ። ከፍተኛ ዘመናዊ ፋብሪካዎች ተቋቋሙ። ሆስፒታሎች ተሠሩ። የቀዳማዊ ኃይለ ሥላሴ ዩኒቨርሲቲ የዓለማያ የእርሻ ኮሌጅ የጎንደር የጤና ኮሌጅ የኢትዮጵያ ዓየር መንገድ ዘመናዊ ፖሊስ ዓየር ኃይል ባሕር ኃይል የምድር ጦር ዘመናዊ እርሻ መገናኛ ቴሌኮሙኒኬሺን መብራት ኃይል ወዘተርፈ። እኒህ ሁሉ የተዋቀሩት በሃምሳ ዓመት ውስጥ ነው።

የግል እርሻ የእንስሳት ርባታ ሁሉ ተጀመረ። ፍራፍሬ ቅጠላ ቅጠል አበባዎች የእንስሳት ውጤቶች የቅባት እህሎች የውጭ ምንዛሪ ማስገኛ ሆኑ። ኢትዮጵያ በታሪኳና በባሕሏ ብቻ ሳይሆን በእርሻም ምርቶቿም መታወቅ ጀመረች። የግል ገበሬዎች የእርሻዎቻቸው ምርቶች በሚሊዮን የሚቆጠሩ ትርፎችን ማካበት ቻሉ። ቤት መሥራት መንገድ መጥረግ ለሥራ መሮጥ የወጣቱ ትውልድ የእውን ሕልም ሆነ። ቢሮዎች እየተተዉ ወደ እርሻ ተወጣ። ልማት ልማት እንደ ሰላምታ ቃላት የእፍ ማሟሻ ሆነ። ቀን ብቻ ሳይሆን ሌሊትም መሥራት ተጀማምሮ ነበር። ያ ወኔ ያ ጀግንነት ያገር ግንባታ በወሬ ኳኳታ በድንገት ተፈታ።

ከዚህ ቀጥሎ ላቀርብላችሁ የምሻው ኢትዮጵያዊ የሆነ ሁሉ የሚሰማው ፀፀት የእግር እሳት የሆነበትን የመከራው የሰቆቃው ዝናም በኢትዮጵያ ምድር እንደ ዶፍ መውረዱን ነው። ይህ ፀፀት ለትውልድና ለታሪክም ነው። ያን የመሠለ የዕድገት ዕንቅስቃሴ በጠላት በረዶ ተመታ። ረገፈ። ከትቢያ ተደባለቀ። ይህ እንዴት ሊሆን ቻለ? ማነው ተጠያቂው? እየተባባሉ

ጣት መቀሠሩ የጠፋውን አያስገኝም። የፈሰሰውን አያፍስም። የሞተውን አያድንም። ግን ክፉ በክፋቱ ደግ በድግነቱ መወሳትና መዘከር የታሪክ ግዴታ ነው።

ቀዳማዊ ኃይለ ሥላሴ ከጋማ ከብት እስከ ጄት ያደረሱ ታላቅና ልዩ የኢትዮጵያ ሕዝብ ባለውለታውና አባቱም ንጉሠ ነገሥቱም ናቸው። ጃንሆይ በሰማኒያ አምስት ዓመታቸው የሚሠሯቸው ሁሉ ሽምግልና ይከላከላቸዋል። ባጠገባቸው የነበሩት ግን የሁኔታዎች ተንከባካቢ መሆን ነበረባቸው። ያ ሳይሆን በመቅረቱ ማንም ይሁን ማን ለጥፋቱ ጀማሪዎች ናቸው።

ዓለም ለሁለት ካምፖች መከፈል ያስነሳው የፖለቲካ ዓውሎ ነፋስ ጣራችንን ወስዶታል። ዛፋችንን መንግሎታል። በአካባቢያችን ተሰግስገው የሚሞተውን በሬ አንጀት ጉበት ለመብላት የሚጠብቁ የጉንብ አሞሮች ሞታችንን አፋጠኑት። ከዚህም ባሻገር መጽሐፍ ቅዱስ ይዘው የመጡት ያአፍሪቃ ነፍሰ በላዎች ተራራው ዝቅ ይበል እያሉ ሰበኩ። ፍቅርን ሳይሆን ጥልን ሰላምን ሳይሆን ሁከትን ሰበኩብን።

ሌሎች ደግሞ ማጭድና መዶሻ ይዘው ብቅ አሉ። ማጭዱ እንኳን ስንዴ ሙጃ የማያጭድ ሆኖ ተገኘ ። ነገር ግን ዕጅ የሚቆርጥ እህል የሚነቅል ሆነ። መዶሻውም እንኳን ብረት ጉሊት የማይፈረክስ እንዲያው የጨርቅ ምስል ብቻ ሆኖ ቀረ። ይህን በደም አበላ የተለወሰ ቀይ ባንዲራ የጭንቅና የሞት ዓርማ ተሸክመው ብቅ አሉ። የሚያሳዩት ምርት በአቡጀዲድ ላይ የተሳለ የሩሲያ ስንዴ ብቻ ነበር። ሕዝቡም ቢቸግረው መቼ ይሆን በሥዕል የምናየውን ስንዴ አገራችን በቅሎ የምንመገበው ሳይሆን የምንመለከተው ብሎ ሲጠይቅ ስልጅ ልጆችህ ነው ኢትዮጵያን የምንገነባው ተብሎ አረፈ። ይህማ ላም አለችኝ በሰማይ ወተቷን የማላይ ተብሎ ተነግሮብሃል ብሎ በታወቀው በአሽሙር መልሱ ተናገረ።

ታዲያ ሕዝቡ በሕይወቱ ከነብር ሲሸሽ በዘንዶ መንገዱ ተዘግቶበት እነሆ እስከዚች ቀን ድረስ የልጆቹ ደም እንደ ነሐሴ ጎርፍ በአደባባይ ይጎርፋል። በረሀብ

በሥራ እጥነት የሞት ሠልፉን ይዞ እየጠበቀ ነው። ይባስ ብሎም ወላጆች በግፍ የተገደሉ ልጆቻቸውን አስከሬን ገዝተው የመቅበር ዕድል አግኝተዋል። እኒህም በጊዜው ዕድለኞች ተብለዋል። ያልታደሉት ግን የልጃቸውን አስከሬን አውሬ በልቶት ያጥንት ስብርባሪ አዩኝ አላዩኝ ብለው ለቃቅመው በልብስ ሳጥኖቻቸው ቋጥረው ሴት ከቀን ያለቀሱ ወላጆችም ነበሩና ሌሎቹ ዕድለኞች ተባሉ። በራሱ አገር በራሱ ሕዝብ ይህን መሳይ ግፍ ሲፈፀም ምን ይባላል? ይህ ትውልድ ይህ ሕዝብ ያሳለፈውና በማሳለፍ ላይ ያለው የሕይወት ጎዳና በኢትዮጵያ ይህ ነው።

የኢትዮጵያ ሕዝብ ኃብት ንብረቱን ተዘረፈ ለመከራ አልፎ ተሠጠ። በመደብ ተከፈለ። በአገሪቱም የሞት ዓዋጅ ታወጀ። ሃይማኖት ባሕል ሥነ ምግባር ወጥተው ተወረወሩ። ተፈጥሮን በቁጥጥራችን ሆነ መፈከሩ። ይሁንና አትምከር ይምከሩ በቆፈሩት ጉድጓድ ሳይገቡም አይቀሩ። እውነት ሆነ። ተፈፀመ። አሁንም የታሪክ መደገም ሐቅ ነውና ሁኔታው ይደገማል።

እንግዲህ እነዚህ «መሪ» ከተባሉ ግን እኔ አልላቸውም። ታሪክም ይከዳቸዋል ብዬ አምናለሁ። የሚሠጣቸው ቦታ ቢኖር ያው የሥራቸውን የሚገልፀውን የጥፋት ዘመን ብሎ ለእነ ሞሶሎኒ ለእነ ግራዚያኒ የመደበውን ይሆናል። የኢትዮጵያም ሕዝብ በዚሁ መልኩ ሲያስታውሰውና ሲዘከረው ይኖራል። አገር መምራት የሕዝብ አደራ የእግዚአብሔርም ፈቃድ ሲወሐዱበት ነበር።

ይህ ያለንበት ዘመን ምን ተብሎ እንደሚነገር እንኳን የሰው ልጆች የመላእክት ቋንቋኳን አይገልፀውም። ዛሬ ልማቱ ሰላሙ አብሮ መኖሩ ሩቅ ዘመን መስሎ ቢታየንም ቅሉ የተፈጥሮ ግዴታና የሰብአዊ ባሕሪያችን ታክሎበት ወደ አንድነቱ እንመጣለን። ያለፈው ታሪካችን ተመልሶና ታድሶ እንደገና ያስተሳስረናል ብለን እናምናለን። የሚታይም ሕልም ነው። ጭቅጭቁ ንትርኩ እርስ በርስ መተረማመሱ መጨራረሱ ሁሉ መቼ ይሆን እንደ ጉም

በኖ እንደ ጤዛ ተኖ የሚጠፋው? ዛሬ ነገ ወይንስ ከነገ ወዲያ? ምኞት ከሆነ አሁንኑ እንላለን።

እንግዲህ አስታውሱ ያ ሃምሳ ዓመት የሥራ ፍሬን ተተኪው ትውልድ እንዲያውቀው እንዲገነዘበው ፍላጎቴና ምኞቴ ነው። ኢትዮጵያውያን ሰላም ወዳጆች ነን። ካልነኩን አንተናኮልም ነበር። የታወቅንበትም ታሪካችን የሚመሠክረው ይህንኑ ነው። ነፃነታችንን ክብራችንን አስከብረን የኖርነውም በዚሁ መልኩ ነው። አሁንም በራሳችን ጥረት አለን።

አብሮ መዋል ማደር አብሮ መብላትና መጠጣት ሁሉ ቀርቶ ሰው እንደ ከብት በሽሃ ተከፋፍሎ በጉረኖ ያሊያም በክልል ታግቶ ማየት ምንኛ ይዘገንናል። የሦስት ሺህ ዓመታት ያንድነት የሥልጣኔ መንግሥት የነበረው ሕዝብ ዛሬ እኔ አንተ አንቺ የሚበባልበት ወቅትና ጊዜ ላይ ወደቀ። በቆሎና ገብስ ይመስል በዘር እንዴት እንለያይ? ይህን ያመጣ የሚያራምድ ቡድንስ በምን ዓይን ቢመለከተው ነው? ተብሎ እንዴት ይጠራል? አማካሪ የሌለው ንጉሥ ያላንድ ዓመት አይነግሥ የሚባለውን ንግርት ባግባቡ ቢጠና ይበጃል እንላለን። ያለበለዚያ ምከረው ምከረው እምቢ ካለ መከራ ይምከረው። አሁንም እንደተጠበቀ ነው።

የሚያሳዝነው በዚህ የመከራ ዘመን ተወልደው በመከራ ላደጉና ላሉ ሁሉ ወጣት ትውልድ ነው። ይህ ትውልድ በእውኑ የወገን ያገር ፍቅር አግኝቷልን? ትምህርቱን ጨርሶ ሥራ የሚያገኝበት አገር በሰቀቀን በጥላቻ በፍርሃትና ሞትሁ ተረፍሁ በሚባልበት አካባቢ ያደገ ትዝታው ምንድን ነው? የነፃነትን ትርጉም ያውቃል? ምስቅልቅሉ ከወጣ ሕይወት ከመኖር ያለመኖር ይሻላል በሚል ውጣ ውረድ ተወጥሮ ያደገ ትውልድ የሚጠበቅበት ፍሬ ምንድን ነው? ይህ ሁኔታ እጅግ አድርጎ ያሳሰበኛል። እንደ አባትነቴም ያስጨንቀኛል።

እኛ ከወላጆቻችን ያገኘነው ፍቅሩ ሥነ ሥርዓቱ ተስፋው ከዚያም አልፎ ተርፎ ያላቸውን ሀብት ከቅርስ እስከ ድቃቂ ሳንቲም ራስ ድረስ ያባት ለልጅ ነበር።

ልጅ ያደገበቱ ቤቱ ባድማው ዛፉ ሁሉም ቅርሳ ቅርሱ ለልጆች ነበር። ከዚያ ዘመን ከዚያ ሕይወት ተገፍተን ተጥለን የወደቅንበትን ትመልከቱት። ዛሬ እንኳን ለልጅ የምናወርሰው እርሥት ቅርስ ሊኖረን የዕለት እንጀራ ከአፋቸው ለማድረግ ጠፍቶ ልጆች በልመናና በጎዳና ኑሮ የወጣትነት ሕይወታቸውን በረኸኛው ተያይዘውት ይገኛሉ።

ተስፋ ሕይወት ቅርስ ነውና አንድ ቀን ከዚህ ማጥ ወጥተው የሰው ልጅ ሊኖር ወደሚገባው የሕይወት ጎዳና ይመለሳሉ ብለን ማሰቡና መመኘቱ ሌላው ቢቀር የወላጅነት ኅሊናችን ያስገድደናል። ልጆቻችንን ያለ አገር ያለ ባሕል ያለ ቋንቋ ያለ ፍቅር ያለ እርሥት ያለ መሪ ጥለናቸው መሄዱ የበደል በደል ይሆንብናልና ወላጆች ለተተኪው ትውልድ ሕይወት አቅጣጫ ማመልከት ታሪካዊና ብሔራዊ ግዴታችን መሆኑ የግዴታ ግዴታ ነው።

የኛ ልጅነትም ሆነ ጎልማሳነት የመንገድ ፍተሻ የቢሮው በር ብርበራ የት ትኖራለህ? የት ትሄዳለህ? መታወቂያህን አሳይ የማናውቃቸውና ያልነበሩ ያላደግንባቸው አሠራሮችና ቋንቋዎች ናቸው። አዲስ ልምድ ልዩ ዝዬና ፈሊጦች ናቸው። ሰው በሰውነቱ እንጂ በተወለደበትና ባደገበት አካባቢ አይታይም አይለካም። ሰዎች ይገናኛሉ ተራሮች ብቻ ናቸው ባሉበት ኖረው የሚቀሩት የሚለው አባባል ትምህርታዊነቱ ለተተኪው ትውልድ ሁሉ ነው። ታዲያ ለዚህ ትውልድ ምን የማይነገረው ምንስ የማይሠጠው ነገር አለ? ከሁሉም ያጣና የነጣ ነውና!

የሦስት ሺህ ዓመት ታሪክ ባለቤትነት በነፃነት የኖረ ተባብሮና ተከባብሮ የነበር አንዱ ከሌላው ተጋብቶና ተዛምዶ ያለና የቆየ መሆኑን ማስረዳት ማስተማር የውዴታ ግዴታ ነው። መንግሥትና ሕዝብ አባትና ልጅ ሆነው የኖሩበት ሕዝቡም መሪዎችን እንደ አባት ያየበት ችግሩን የሚያስረዳበት ያጣውን ጠይቆ የሚያገኝበት ለመልካም ሥራው የሚሸለምበት ዘመን ነበር። ይኼውም የዓይን ምሥክርነት የምንሠጠውና የምንናገርለት የቀዳማዊ ኃይለ ሥላሴ ዘመን ነው። ስለ

ቀዳማዊ ኃይለ ሥላሴ ታላቅነት ብልህነት አስተዋይነትና ብልህ አመራር የዓለም ጋዜጦች የታሪክ መዛግብት ሁሉ አድናቆታቸውን ገልፀውላቸዋል። ይህም የታሪክ ትዝታ ነው።

ጃንሆይ በአሜሪካ

ጃንሆይ ለመጀመሪያ ጊዜ አሜሪካንን ሲጎበኙ የዘመኑ ፕሬዚዴንት ፍራንክሊን ሩዝቬልት ነበሩ። ከሳቸውም ጋር ስለ ኢትዮጵያ ልማትና የወደፊት እርምጃ በኋይት ሀውስ ተነጋግረዋል። ጃንሆይ ወደ አሜሪካ በመጡበት ጊዜ ሁሉ ስለ ጥቁር አሜሪካኖች ነፃነት ሳይወያዩና ሳያሳስቡ ያለፉበት ጊዜ አልነበረም። ይህ የንጉሠ ነገሥቱ ማሳሰቢያ ለማርቲን ሉተር ኪንግ የነጻነት እንቅስቃሴ መቅድም ነበር። የእግዚአብሔር ፈቃድም ሆኖ ፈጻሚ አግኝቷል። በሁለተኛ ጉብኝታቸው ጊዜ በ 1952 ዓ. ም ዩናይትድ ስቴትስ አፍ አሜሪካን በጎበኙበት ወቅት ለአሜሪካኑ ኮንግረስ ንግግር አድርገዋል።

ያን ዘመን በአሜሪካን ታሪክ የተመለከትነው እንደሆነ የአፍሪቃ አኅጉር በቅኝ ገዥዎቻቸው ሰንሰለት ታሥረው የነበሩበት በተለይም ጥቁሮች በከፍተኛ ደረጃ ተለይተው ነጮች በደረሱበት የማይታዩበት የዘር መድልዎ የነበረበት ዘመን ነበር። በዚያን ጊዜና ወቅት ነበር ጃንሆይ እስካሁን ለማንም አፍሪቃዊ ኤሲያዊና የመካከለኛው ምሥራቅ መሪዎች ተደርጎ የማያውቅ የክብር አቀባበል በዚሁ አገር ርዕሰ ከተማ በዋሺንግተን ዲሲ በኋይት ሐውስ ቤተ መንግሥት የተደረገላቸው። ይህ ለኢትዮጵያውያን ሁሉ የተደረገ ክብርና ኩራት ነበር።

ጃንሆይ ለኢትዮጵያ ሕዝብ ያደረጉት ጥረትና ድካም የሚተች የሚነቀፍ አይደለም መሆንም አይገባውም። ለኢትዮጵያ ሥልጣኔና ዕድገት ከልብ የደከሙና የጣሩ እውነተኛ መሪና አባት ነበሩ። ነቢይ

በአገሩ አይከብርም እንደ ተባለው ሁሉ ሆኖ ከሳቸው ዘንድ ሥልጣን ለመንጠቅ ያቆበቆቡት ጠላቶቻችን ጊዜውንና ሁኔታውን ተጠቅመው ሲያሳስቱና ሲያደቡ የኖሩበት ኢትዮጵያን የማጥፋቱ ሁኔታ ተሳክቶላቸው በመጀመሪያ በተማሪው ግርግር ቀጥሎም መግደልና ማጥፋት በሚችለው የማጥፊያው መሣሪያ ባለውና በዕጁ በያዘው ለዚሁም ሙያ በሠለጠነው የኀብረተ ሰብ ክፍል ሥልጣኑ እንዲወድቅ ተደረገ። በያዘው መሣሪያም የኢትዮጵያን ተተኪ ትውልድና አሉ የሚባሉ ምሁራንና ያገር ሽማግሎችን ፈጀ።

እጅግ አድርጎ የሚጸጽተውና የሚቆረቁረው ከዚያ ዓይነቱ አስተዳደር ወጥተን አሁን ከደረስንበት ደረጃ ላይ መገኘታችን ነው። የወደፊቱም አቅጣጫችን ምን መስሎ እንደሚጓዝ በትንቢት ይያዝልኝ። ታዲያ የሚያስገርመው በዚህ በዘመነ ሳይንስ የበይ ተመልካች ሆነን እንዳንቀር ግንዛቢያችንን በር ዘግተን እንዳንቀመጥ አደራዬ ጽኑ ነው።

የአዳማ ልጆች ትዝታ

እስቲ ወደ ልጅነት ትዝታዬ ልውሰዳችሁ
ላንዴና ለመጨረሻ ጊዜ ልመልሳችሁ
ጓደኞቼ ወዳጆቼ ፍቀዱልኝ።
ያን የጥንቱን በዓይነ ኅሊና እዩልኝ
በሙሉ አካባቢውን ቃኙልኝ።
ግራና ቀኙን ላይና ታቹን ተመልከቱልኝ
ሳትፈተሹ ከዳማ አዲስ አበባ ደርሶ መልስ
የመጣችሁ
ሳትከፍሉ መልካ ጅሎ የሄዳችሁ
በባቡሩ ጣቢያ የተጫወታችሁ የቧረቃችሁ
ሼፍ ዴትሬኑን በጋሼ ብቻ ያባበላችሁ
ወንድም መስሳችሁ በነጻ የተጓዛችሁ
ያንን ፍቅር የት አደረሳችሁ?
ዘወርወር ብሎ ማየቱ ምነው ተሳናችሁ?

እንዳሁኖቹ ልጆች ካሁን አሁን በጥይት ሳትሉ
ተመታሁ
ከላይ እታች ከውስጥ ከውጭ የፉለላችሁ
ተናገሩ መሥክሩ የነበረውን እባካችሁ
እናንተኮ ናችሁ የነበራችሁ።
እናንት የዛሬ አባቶች የትላንቱ ልጆች
የዛሬ ዛሬማ ስደተኞች
ያሊያም ከሥራ ተባራሪዎች
ተነሡ ተናገሩ መሥክሩ እኅት ወንድሞች።
ለማን ብላችሁ ተናገሩ መሥክሩ
እንደልጅነታችን እውነት ተናገሩ
የፈለገው ይሁን በመሸበት እደሩ
ግና ግና ያያችሁትን የነበራችሁበትን አውሩ
ሐሰተኞች በዝተዋል ድንጋዩን ዳቦ ነው ብለዋል
ጤፍ ከማይበቅልበት ጭድ ከመሩ
ያላዩትን አስመስለው አወሩ
የዘመኑ ወፍጯችን የቆመው
ሲከካና ሲፈጭ ሌሊቱን ሙሉ የሚያድረው
የሐሰት ወሬ የቅጥፈት ዜናኮ ነው።
እናንት አብረን የአዳልን በረሀ በእግር
የተጓዝነው
የኩሬ ውሀ ተግተን ያደግነው።
እንደ ፈሪ ንብረታችንን ተቀምተን ዝም ያልነው
ምነውኮ የማናስመልሰው?
ዝምታው ችልታው ምንድን ነው?
ተነሡ እንነሣ ውርዱ እንውረድ
ሞትኮ የማይቀር ነው በውድም በግድ።

አባት ያቆየው ለልጅ ይበጀው

የሰው ልጅ በታሪክ በአኖኗር አሁን ያለበትን መልክና ቅርጽ ከመያዙ በፊት አብሮ መኖሩ ሁሉ በአመክሮና በተዘክሮ ከብዙ ጊዜ ሙከራ የተገኘ ለመሆኑ የሰው ልጅ አመጣጥና ታሪክ ተመራማሪ ሊቃውንት ተገቢውን ማስረጃ አቅርበውለታል። እንግዲህ ይህ በእንዲህ እንዳለ ወደ አገራችን ታሪክ የተመለስን እንደሆነ ብዙ የምንዘከራቸው ጉዳዮች እንዳሉ መገንዘብ ግዴታችን ይሆናል። ይህስ ከሆነ ዘንድ እጅግ አድርገን የምናተኩርበቸው ዐበይት ቁምነገሮች እንዳሉ የመገንዘብ ግዴታ መኖሩን መረዳት ይኖርብናል።

ይህን ካልን ዘንድ ወደ ንባቡ ተልኮ እናምራ። ይህን ለመናገር ያስገደደን ያለንበት ሁኔታና ሂደት ጉዳይ ነው። ዛሬ ወዴት እያመራን ነው? ምንስ እየተደረገ ነው? የሚሉትን ጥያቄዎች ያነሣን እንደሆነ የሚሠጡትን መልሶች ስንመረምር የሚከተሉትን ፍሬ ኃሳቦች እናገኛለን። የዛሬ ወጣቶች እንዴት ወዴት እያመሩና ምንስ እየሠሩ ነው? ይህን በጆሮ ከመሥማቱም ባሻገር በዓይን የምናየው ጉዳይ ነው። ስለሆነም ሳይቃጠል በቅጠል ነውና ሳይርቅ በቅርብ ይህን የተፈጠረውን ችግር ማስወገድና ማስተካከል የእያንዳንዳችን ታላቅ ኃላፊነት ይሆናል።

የአገር ፍቅር ባህል በራስ መኩራት መመካትና ይሉኝታ ባሁኑ ትውልድ እንዴት ይታያሉ? የአገር ጉዳይ እንዲሁ ዝም ብሎ የማያዩት መሆኑን በጥሞና አሁንም መገናዘብ ይገበዋል። ያአገር ጉዳይ እንዲሁ እንደ ፈረስ ሣር በየቦታው ራሱ ከእግር እግሩ ከራስ ሆኖ ተነስንሶ ይገኛል። መብላት ለመኖር እንጂ ለመብላት መኖር መሆን የለበትም። ይህ ከሆነ ሕይወትን እንዲሁ ያለ ምግባረ ሠናይ ማሣለፍ መሆኑ ነው። እንዲህስ ማድረግ ይገባል ወይ?

በአገራችን በተለምዶው ልጅ ለወላጁ እውነተኛና ፍጹም ነው። አሁን ግን እንደሚታየው ወላጅን አሳልፎ መሥጠት በልጆች ተለምዷል። ይህ ዓይነት ተግባር ሲፈጸም ታይቶም አይታወቅም ነበር። እንግዲህ የሚሆነውን ሁሉ ያየነውና የታዘብነው ነው። ይህ ዓይነቱ አሠራር በታሪክ ተደግሟል ቢባል እንኳን አሠራሩ እየቅል ነው። ታሪኩም ይህ ነው። በአሥራ ዘጠነኛው መቶ ክፍለ ዘመን የዓፄ ቴዎድሮስን መንግሥት ለመጣል ሲባል በጄኔራል ናፒየር የሚመራው የእንግሊዝ ጦር ሠራዊትን መርቶ ማስገባት ከገበና ማጋለጥ ይቆጥራል? ወይስ አይቆጠርም? ይህን ለብዙኃኑ ኢትዮጵያዊ እተወዋለሁ።

ባገራችን ለብዙ ሺህ ዓመታት ነገሥታት ሲፈራረቁ እርስ በርሳቸው ቢዋጉና ቢጣሉም ተከታዮቻቸው ላሸነፈው በማደር የአገራችን ክብርና ኩራት አንዴም በውጭ ኃይል ሳይደፈር በአፍሪቃ ብቻ ሳይሆን በመላው ዓለም ተደናቂነት አግኝታ መኖሯ ለዛሬዎቹ ተረካቢዎች የኩራትና የአለኝታ ሙዳይ ሆና ተገኝታለች። እኛም ባልሠራነውና ባላፈሰስነው ደም ባልከሰከስነው አጥንት በነኝሁ አባቶቻችንና አያቶቻችን ደምና አጥንት በመመካት ስለነፃነታችን አንገታችንን ሳንደፋ በኩራት ኖረናል። የወደፊቱን ገና አላወቅንም።

ለነገሩማ ልጅ ሲያጠፋ በአባት በእናት ይመከር ነበር። ነገር ግን ያ ወግና ማዕርግ አሁን ተለውጧል። ለጥፋት ለብዙ ዘመን ለጥፋታችን አሰፍስፈው ይጠባበቁ የነበሩት የውጭ ኃያላን ወጥመድ ውስጥ ገባን። ኢትዮጵያ ከዚህ ዓይነቱ መሠናክል ሳትገባ ከቆየች በኋላ በተካሄደው ዘመቻና ሤራ ሰውን ከሰው ሃይማኖትን ከሃይማኖት ለያዩት። ይህም ቀደም ሲል በተነደፈው ፕላንና ሤራ በ1930ኛው ዓመት ተሞክሮ ነበር። ሆኖም በዘመኑ የነበሩት አያቶቻችን አባቶቻችን እንደ ዛሬዎቹ ወጣቶች ኬሚስትሪን ቲሪጎኖሜትሪን አልጀብራንና የመሳሰሉትን ባይማሩም ለሀገራቸውና ለወገናቸው ለአንድነታቸው ቆራጦች

ነበሩ። የአንድነት ዓርማቸውም እንደ ብረት ግድግዳ ጠንካራ ነበር።

ንጉሡ በጦር ሜዳ እንደ ተራ ሰው ከተዋጉ በኋላ ከሠለጠነው ከጠላት ጦር ጋር ባዶ እግሩን በወጨፎ በናስ ማሰርና ምንሽር ጠመንጃ ተዋግቶ የማይሸነፍና የማይበገር ሆነ። በሰማይ ላይ የሚወርድበትን የመርዝ ጢስ መቋቋም አልቻለም። ብዙ ወገናችንም ደከመ። በዚህን ጊዜ ነው ንጉሠ ነገሥቱ ወደ ጀኔቫ እንዲሄዱ የተወሰነው። ምክንያቱም ጦሩ ከወደቀና ከደከመ በኋላ ዕጅ መሥጠት የመጨረሻው ኢትዮጵያ የማትወደውን ውርደት መከናነብ ስለሚሆን ንጉሠ ነገሥቱ ዕጃቸውን እንዳይሠጡ ተደርጎ ወደ ስደት ተሸጋገሩ።

እንዲህም ሆኖ ቢሄዱም በሀገሩ የቀረው ጀግናው ኢትዮጵያዊ ሴት ወንድ ሳይል ተዋጋ። በዱር በገደሉ ባመቸው ሁኔታ ጠላትን መግቢያ መውጫ አሳጠው። ንጉሠ ነገሥቱም በፖለቲካ የዓለም ሕዝብ በነቢይነት እስኪያደንቃቸው ድረስ ታገሉ። በጄኔቫ የፖለቲካ ጦርነት በማድረግ በመጨረሻም የድል ባለቤት ሆንን። ኢትዮጵያውያን ለኩራትና ለአንድነት በቃን።

ታዲያ አሁንም ያልተኙልን ጠላቶቻችን ማለያየትን ሥራዬ ብለው ጀመሩ። በዚህም የተነሣ ንጉሡን ከወጣቱ ትውልድ እንዲለያዩ አደረጉ። ወጣቱ በጨቅላ አዕምሮው ለኢትዮጵያ የሚበጅ የልማት ግስጋሴ እንዲያደርግ የተከፈተለትን የትምህርት ገበታ ትቶ ተሠናከለ። የውጭዎቹ የሚነዙትን የሀሰት የማለያየት ፕሮፓጋንዳ ተቀበለ።

አሁን እንዳለበት ተለያየ። ተከፋፈለ። ተሠነጣጠቀ። ከመጠናከር መዳከምን ከሀብት ድህነት ከፍቅር ጥላቻን አበረከተ። ከማግኘት ማጣትን ከባላገርነት ስደተኛነትን አስከተለ። ከማወቅና ከመመራመር ይልቅ ድንቁርናን አገኘ። ላም ባልዋለበት ኩበት ለቀማ እንዲሉ የማያውቁት አዋቂ መስሎ መታየትን ጀመሩ። ከክብር ውርደትን ከወግ ይልቅ ሥርዓተ አልበኛነትንና የመሳሰሉትን በደንብ

እንዲቀሰምና ዋጋ የሌለው ሕብረተ ሰብ እንዲሆን ጠላቶቻችን አደረጉ።

ይህንም የተመለከትን እንደሆነ ሃይማኖት የሞኝነት የዋዛ የፌዝዛ ነገር ነው ሲሉ ወጣቱን ሠበኩት። ሃይማኖት በኢትዮጵያውያን ዘንድ የሥነ ምግባር ምንጭና መገኛ መሆኑን ስለሚገነዘቡት ወጣቱን ከሃይማኖቱ ከተላቀቀ ወደሚፈልጉት አቅጣጫ ለመምራት እንደሚቻል በጥሞና ደህና አድርገው ስለሚያውቁ ነው። ስለሆነም እንደተመኙትና እንደፈለጉትም ማድረግ ቻሉ። ስለዚህ ለወጣቱ በሠፊው የተሠበከለት ሃይማኖት ማደንዘዣ ዕፅ ነው የሚል ነበር።

ስለዚህ ክርስቲያኑ በክርስትና እምነቱ እንዲያፍር አድርገውታል። እንዲሁም የቀሩት ሁሉ ማለት እስላሙ ከመስጊዱ እንዲወገድ ተደርጓል። ይህም ሲሆን ከነበረው ወግና ሥርዓት አስወጥተውታል። እንግዲህ በጠቅላላው ማዕርጉን ክብሩን እያጣ ሄደላቸው። ከዚህም የተነሣ ጠንካራው እምነቱ አንድነቱ ተቦረቦረ። ስለ አገር ያለውና የነበረው ፍቅር ከላዩ ላይ እንዲነሳ ተደረገ።

በልማት ስም የነበረውን ሥርዓት አፍርሰው ለውጭው ገበናችንን ከፍተን ተውን። ፈረንሣይ እንግሊዝ ሩሲያ አሜሪካ ደርሶ የመጣ ወጣት ሁሉ እንደሊቅ ተቆጥሮ አባት እናት ቢናገሩት ከወዴት ይሰማ። ወላጆች ያላዋቂ ሆኖ መታየትና መቆጠር እንደ ልምድ ተወሰደ። ታዲያ ሁሉ ነገር ለጥራዝ ነጠቁ ወጣት ተሠጠና አሁን ያለንበት ሁኔታ ላይ ደርሰናል። በዚሁ ሁናቴ እንዲሁ እንቀጥል ወይንስ ምን ይሻላል? አሁንም መፍትሔ ከመሻት አልቦዘንም። ጉዳዩ የጋራ ነውና ሁላችንም እንረባረብበት እላለሁ።

ታሪካችንን እንዘንጋ። ግርማዊ ቀዳማዊ ኃይለ ሥላሴ ንጉሠ ነገሥታችን ከጦርነቱ ወጥተው ለአውሮጳ ጉዞ ወደ ጂቡቲ ሲደርሱ ጣሊያኖች አዲስ አበባን ያዙ። በዚህን ጊዜ ነው ይባላል የሞሶሊን ሚስት የኢጣሊያን ባለሥልጣኖችን ጠርታ ስለ አዲስ አበባ

መያዝ ስትጠይቅ ባለሥልጣናቱ ኢትዮጵያ ያለውን ወኪላቸውን ጠይቀው የተረዱትን ሲነግሯት የተናገረችው እንዲህ የሚል ነበር። ለመሆኑ ያገሪቱን ዋና ከተማ ያዛችሁ ኃይለ ሥላሴንሳ? ምን አደረጋችሁ? እሱን ካልያዛችሁ ልፋታችሁ ሁሉ ከንቱ ነው። ይልቁንም በዚህ ሳቢያ ሌሎች የአፍሪቃ አገሮች ነፃ እንዳይወጡ እንፈራለን አለች ይባላል። እንደተባለውም በጄኔቫ ያደረጉት ንግግር አቤቱታና እውነተኛን ፍርድ መጠየቅ እስከ ዛሬ ድረስ እየተደነቀ ይኖሯል። መተኪያም አልተገኘለትም።

የሞሶሎኒ ሚስት እንዳላቸው ኢትዮጵያ ነፃነቷን ከመለሰች በኋላ ጃንሆይ ለኬንያ ለታንዛንያና ለኡጋንዳ ልዩ ወጭ መድበው ኢትዮጵያ ባላት ችግርና በኤኮኖሚ ጉሥቁልና ወደ ኋላ ሳይሉ ለጆሞ ኬንያታ ለጁሊዩስ ኔሬሬና ለአሁኑ ለደቡብ አፍሪቃ መሪ ለኔልሰን ማንዴላ ሳይቀር በየወሩ $300,000.00 የአሜሪካን ዶላር ለእያንዳንዳቸው እያከፋፈሉ በፖለቲካ እየተዋጉላቸው ነፃነት ያስገኙ ጀግናን ንጉሥ ከሕዝቡ በቀላሉ ማጣላትና ማለያየት ማዋረድ ለታላላቅ ነኝ ባይ መንግሥታት ትልቅ አጥጋቢ ውጤትና ዓላማ ነበር።

በቀላሉ በአሥራ ዘጠኝ መቶ ዓርባ ዓ. ም. ጥቁር አሜሪካኖች ከፍተኛ የዘር መድልዎ እየተደረገባቸው ባለበት ወቅት ነበር ጃንሆይ በኋይትሀውስ (White House) የተስተናገዱት። ይህ እንዲሁ የተገኘ ክብር እንዳልሆነ ልንገነዘበው ይገባል። ታሪክ ነውና በዚያን ዘመን ጥቁሮች በበታችነት የሚታዩበት ጊዜ ነበርና ነው። ጥቁሮች በሰው ልጅነታቸው የዕኩልነት መብት ተነፍጓቸው በሚንገላቱበት ወቅት ጃንሆይ ታሪክ እንደሚያስታውሰው ለጥቁሮች መብት ሳይጠይቁና ሳያነጋግሩ ያለፉበት ሰዓት እንዳልነበር ማስገንዘብ እወዳለሁ። ታዲያ በዚያ ዘመን ነበር ዓፄ ኃይለ ሥላሴ ለአሜሪካ የክብር ዕንግዳ የነበሩት። ይህ ክብር የኢትዮጵያውያን ብቻ ሳይሆን የመላው ጥቁር አፍሪቃዊ ሁሉ ነበር ቢባል ያምራል። ያኮራል።

አንቱም ያሰኛል። ያን እስታውሰን መለስ ስንል አሁን የት ነን? እንዴትስ እያደረግን ነው?

የአሜሪካን ሕዝብ ወይም አሜሪካዊ ባለሥልጣን ለማንም ዕጅ አይነሳም ሲባል ለጃንሆይ ግን ዕጅ መንሳታቸው እነሆ በፎቶ ግራፍ በተደገፈ ማሥረጃ ዕጅ ከፍንጅ አቅርበናል።

ሌላም ወግ ልንገራችሁ። ንግሥት ኤልሳቤጥ በአፍሪቃ ጉብኝት ሲያደርጉ ሁሉም እየተንበረከኩ ዕጅ ነስተዋቸዋል። ነገር ግን የጉብኝታቸው አቅጣጫ ወደ ኢትዮጵያ ይሆናል። ኢትዮጵያም ይደርሳሉ። ከዚያም ጃንሆይ ሊቀበሏቸው ኤርፖርት ይደርሳሉ። ከአውርፕላን ንግሥት ኤልሳቤጥ ያርፋሉ። ከዚያም ለጃንሆይ በርከክ ብለው ዕጅ ይነሳሉ። ይህ ጉዳይ ከፍተኛ መነጋገሪያ ርዕሰ ጉዳይ ሆኖ ለንደን ሲደርሱ ንግሥቲቷ ለምን ለዓፄ ኃይለ ሥላሴ ዕጅ ነሡ? ይባላሉ። ይህን የሚጠይቀው የእንግሊዝ ፓርላማ ነው። ወቀሳውም ጠበቅ ያለ ነው ይባላል። ንግሥቲቱ የሠጡት መልስ ግን እንዲህ የሚል ነበር። «ታሪክን ልንሸፍን አንችልም። ኢትዮጵያ ቀደምት አገር ከመሆኗም በላይ ንጉሡ ግርማቸው ያስፈራል።»

ስለዚህ በመጠኑም ቢሆን ይህችን ማስታወሻ ከፎቶግራፋቸው ጋር ለአንባቢያን አውጥቻለሁ። የታሪክ ምሁር ግን ያለመሆኔ ከወዲሁ ይያዝልኝ። ታሪኩን ወይም ማስታወሻውን አንብበው የበለጠ መረጃ መፈለግ የአንባብያንና የኢትዮጵያውያን ኃላፊነት ነው። ነገር ግን የሌለ ታሪክ ከመፍጠርና ራስን ዝቅ ከማድረግ እንቆጠብ። ጥናታዊ ምርምር እናድርግ። ያለንን ታሪክ እናጥና። እናጠናክር። ኑሮአችንን እናሻሽል። በፍቅር በአንድነት እንጠናከር። አሉባልታን ባልተረጋገጠ ሁኔታ ወሬን ከማጋነን እውነት ይዞ መንዝን እንምረጥ። ከወሬ ይልቅ ለሥራ እንሽቀዳደም። በትንሹና በትልቁ ከመለያየት ተነጋግሮ መግባባት መፈቃቀድን ልምድ እናድርግ።

የዛሬ ዓርባ ዓመትና መቶ ዓመት ወደኋላ ብንቆጥር ከጋሬጣ ታግሎ ጭራሮ ለቅሞ በባዶ እግሩ

የሚንከራተተው ኢትዮጵያዊ አሁንም ከዚያው ከነበረበት ላይ ነው። ወዴትም ፈቀቅ አላለም። አሁንም የባላገሯ ሴት የፈጫይ ፈጭታ የጋጋሪ ጋግራ በኩበት ጭስ ዓይኗ ያሞጨሞጨው ኢትዮጵያዊቷ እዚያው ናትኮ! ይህንን ስንቶቻችን ነን የምናውቀው? ይህንን መለወጥ ስንችል ነው እኛ ልንኮራ የሚገባን። ያለበለዚያ የሚሆነው ትለብሰው የላት ትከናነበው አማራት ነው።

በመጨረሻም ልጠይቅ የምፈልገው አባቶቻችን ያቆዩልን ብልሃት አስታራቂነት ጥበብ ወዴት ደረሰ? ወዳጅ ከወዳጅ ቢጣላ አስታራቂዎች ነበሩ። ሰው እንኳ ቢጋደል ወግና ማዕረግን ይዘው ይቅር ለእግዚአብሔር የሚያሰኙ ኢትዮጵያውያን ነበሩ። ዛሬ የመጣው ፈሊጥ የተጣሉት ሰዎች ቁጭ ብለው ተነጋግረው ራሳቸው ይፈቱታል ይባላል። ያልዘሩት ይበቅላል እንዴ? እልሃችን ቁጭታችንስ? ወዴት ተረስቶ?

ከመቶ አንድ ኢትዮጵያዊ አሜሪካ መጥቶ ቴሌቪዥን ዓየና ከዚህ አገር ኖረና የአባት የናቱን ፈለግ ረሳ ማለት ነው? ይህ ሁሉ የማይሆን ነው። ሰው እንሁን የሰውነት ሥራ እንሥራ። የሚበጀው ይህ ነውና! ወደኛው ወደ ኢትዮጵያዊነቱ እንመለስ። ወደ ሀገራችን ልማድና ሥርዓት እናዘንብል። አገራችን ገብተን ለመኖር ምኞትና ፍላጎቱ ይኑረን። አንድ እንሁን። ይህን ለማድረግና ለመፈፀም እንትጋ። ባህላችንን እያስታወስን እንከባበር። እኛነታችንን ከተጠነቀቅንበትና ካከበርነው ብቻ ነው የምንኮራበት። የሌላው ባህል የባዳ ነው። የኛ አይሆንም። የኛም ለነሱ አይሆንም። ባጭሩ ጥሪዬን የማቀርበው እንከባበር እንስማማ እንግባባ አንድ እንሁን እንፈቃቀር ሰላም እንፍጠር ለልማት ለብልጽግና እንነሣ ለማለት ነው።

ተፈፀመ

Haile Selassie

Emperor of Ethiopia
1930 - 1974

A photographic presentation of one of the most outstanding world leaders of the Twentieth Century

Royal treatment for His Majesty traveling to and from the United States, 1952

Ceremony of the departure by the Emperor and Empress of Ethiopia.

The royal couple arrive at the Addis Ababa Airport after their US visit and (below) greet officials at a special welcoming event.

Foreign dignitaries greet Her Majesty Empress Mennen.

The American Ambassador to Ethiopia, Dr. Simonson, bowing and saluting the Emperor and Empress in traditional Ethiopian style.

Motorcade from the airport brings His Majesty Haile Selassie and entourage to the imperial palace in Addis Ababa.

An Emperor in touch with his people

Emperor Haile Salassie walking unguarded in his city, observing the progress Ethiopia has made during the years of his rule.

The Emperor liked to visit farms and businesses owned by Ethiopians who were helping to raise the standard of living for families in the country, including an inspection tour, shown here, of the author's poultry farm.

The Emperor lays the cornerstone for the first university in the history of Ethiopia, November 2, 1950.

Her Majesty Empress Mennen attending services at the Holy Trinity Church in Addis Ababa, 1952.

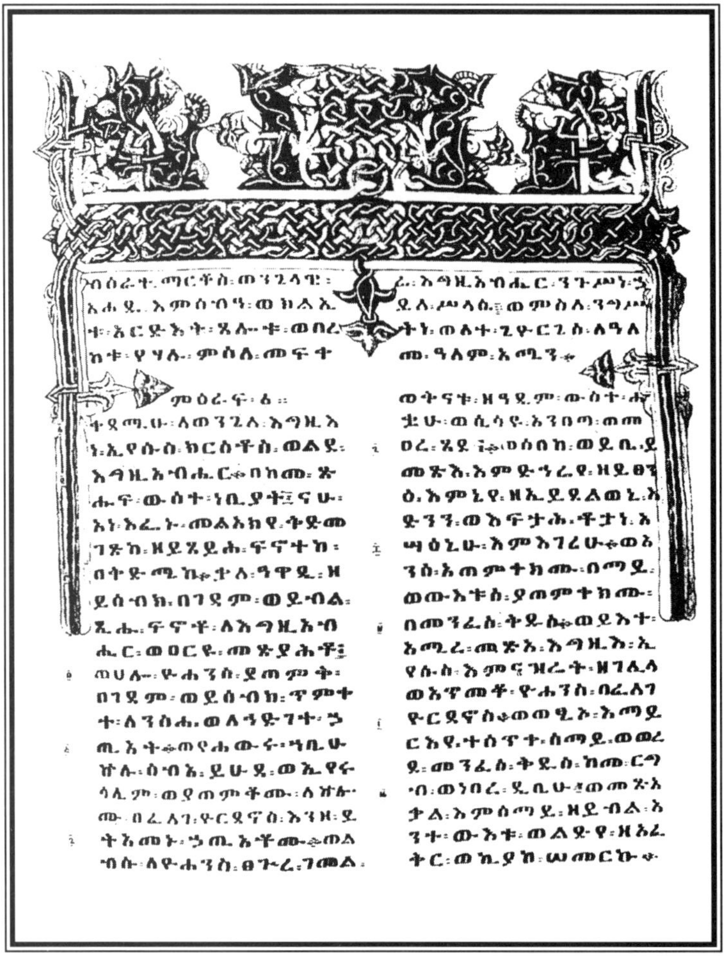

The ancient Ge'ez language is the only African language in script, shown here in a copy of a page from an Ethiopian Bible donated to the Truman Library Collection by Emperor Haile Selassie.

Invading forces and world conflicts occupy the energy of the Emperor—and his country

General Wingate, the Emperor's chief military adviser, and Haile Selassie meet in northern Ethiopia near the border with Sudan to map out a strategy for driving the invading Italian troops from the area in 1936.

The American delegation meets with Emperor Haile Selassie in 1941 to seek military assistance in meeting the challenge of the war.

The entire American delegation poses on the palace steps with the Emperor. From left: F. N. Polangin, Captain Conrad, Lt. Col. Baughey, Colonels Bishop and Clark, George Strompl, Captain Powers and Teferra Worq. These pictures were the first official photographs taken after Ethiopia became a fighting member of the United Nations.

Colonels Bishop (left) and Clark pore over official papers with the Emperor during the American delegation's visit to Ethiopia.

HAILE SELASSIE: A PHOTOGRAPHIC PRESENTATION

His Majesty, Emperor Hale Selassie, prepares to speak to the people of Ethiopia via a radio broadcast from Addis Ababa.

Side by side, Americans and Ethiopians, led by Emperor Haile Selassie, mourn the Ethiopian soldiers who died in the Korean war of the 1950s.

The Betrayal of Ethiopia

Three young Ethiopians (below) reflect on the sacrifice their country made in the Korean War, memorialized in this statue in New York City.

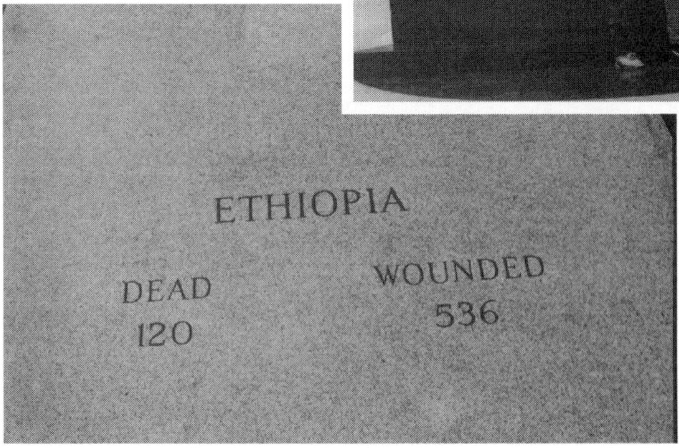

Making friends in the United States

Henry G. Bennett (back row, center) and Emperor Haile Selassie attend a reception for faculty and staff members and children of the Oklahoma A&M University, 1950.

The Emperor at a state reception in his honor by the Mayor of San Francisco, 1952.

The Emperor gives his autograph to a Korean war veteran at a veterans' hospital in San Francisco.

San Francisco's Mayor Robison thanks Emperor Haile Selassie for the gift of an elephant tusk, 1952.

His Majesty presents a gold cross to the St. Paul church in Minnesota.

After being greeted by Allan Pomari of the Boeing Aircraft Factory at the Seattle airport (left), Haile Selassie gets a close-up look at how airplanes are manufactured in the United States.

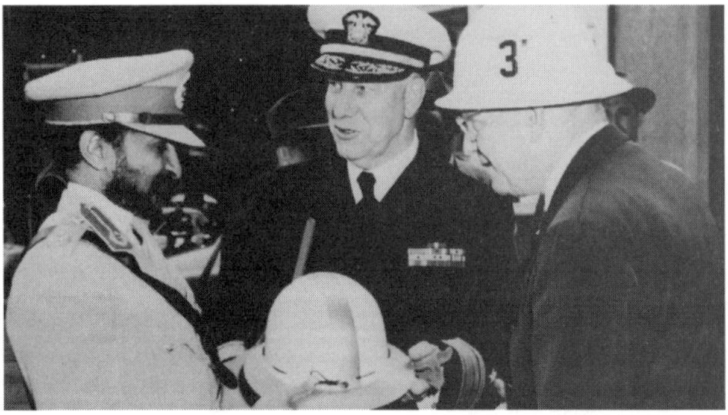

After touring the Boeing plant, His Majesty visited a shipyard in Seattle.

Ethiopia's emperor takes time from his busy schedule in the US to greet a young Ethiopian student attending the University of California at Berkely.

Shaking the hand of an American herdsman in Chicago.

While visiting the United States, Emperor Haile Selassie participates in a review of the troops at a naval installation.

Three Ethiopian leaders return a military salute in the US: His Imperial Majesty Haile Selassie, in front; the crown prince Asfawwessenn on the left and Prince Makonnen Duke of Harar, center.

A world leader among his peers

February 13, 1945: Emperor Haile Selassie and US President Franklin D. Roosevelt confer aboard a US warship.

Courtesy Dwight D. Eisenhower Library

May 25, 1954: America's First Lady Mamie Eisenhower welcomes the Emperor to the United States along with President Dwight D. Eisenhower, right.

Courtesy Dwight D. Eisenhower Library

Emperor Haile Selassie with President and Mrs. Eisenhower at the White House Rose Garden, thanking the Americans for their friendship to Ethiopia and their assistance in developing the country.

Courtesy Dwight D. Eisenhower Library

The Emperor and President Eisenhower at the conclusion of Haile Selassie's 1954 visit to the US.

Portrait of Emperor Haile Selassie inscribed to President Dwight D. Eisenhower.

Courtesy Dwight D. Eisenhower Library

Reviewing the troops with Vice President Richard M. Nixon.

The Kennedy visit, October 1 1963

Photo ST-C307-5-63, John F. Kennedy Library

Official visit to Washington DC, October 1, 1963.

Photo ST-C307-4-63, John F. Kennedy Library

Photo KN-C-30060, John F. Kennedy Library

The Emperor greets America's First Family on October 1, 1963, led by President John F. Kennedy, far left. The leopard coat worn by Mrs. John F. Kennedy was a gift from Emperor Haile Selassie. Little John Jr. stands facing the camera near his mother, and Carolyn is standing to the right. The girl shaking hands with the Emperor is an unidentified playmate of Carolyn's.

Photo ST-C307-11-63, John F. Kennedy Library

The Kennedy visit, continued

Photo KN-C-30045, John F. Kennedy Library

Photo KN-C-30065, John F. Kennedy Library

Photo AR 8150 T, John F. Kennedy Library

Above: At Union Station in Washington, DC with, from left, Ethiopian Princess Ruth Desta, Jacqueline Kennedy, the Emperor, and President John F. Kennedy. The next month after this photo event, on November 22, 1963, the President was assassinated.

Photo KN-C-30046, John F. Kennedy Library

Photo AR 8150P, John F. Kennedy Library

Photo ST-C307-3-63, John F. Kennedy Library

Scenes from the John F. Kennedy funeral procession

Photo PX 65-105:539, John F. Kennedy Library

Photo AR 8255-2R, John F. Kennedy Library

John F. Kennedy funeral continued

Photo ST-C 422-97-63, John F. Kennedy Library

Photo PX 65-105:538, John F. Kennedy Library

Emperor Haile Selassie with President Richard Nixon and the First lady after a White House reception, July 8, 1969.

Haile Selassie after a state visit with President Richard Nixon on the Emperor's last visit to the United States, 1972.

Photo by Yoichi R. Okamato, courtesy the LBJ Library Collection

Official military reception by US President Lyndon B. Johnson and the First Lady is typical of the honor and respect Emperor Haile Selassie enjoyed during his reign in Ethiopia.

Appendix I: APPEAL TO THE LEAGUE OF NATIONS

I, Haile Selassie I, Emperor of Ethiopia, am here today to claim that justice which is due to my people, and the assistance promised to it eight months ago, when fifty nations asserted that aggression had been committed in violation of international treaties.

There is no precedent for a Head of State himself speaking in this assembly. But there is also no precedent for a people being victim of such injustice and being at present threatened by abandonment to its aggressor. Also, there has never before been an example of any Government proceeding to the systematic extermination of a nation by barbarous means, in violation of the most solemn promises made by the nations of the earth that there should not be used against innocent human beings the terrible poison of harmful gases. It is to defend a people struggling for its age-old independence that the head of the Ethiopian Empire has come to Geneva to fulfill this supreme duty, after having himself fought at the head of his armies.

I pray to Almighty God that He may spare nations the terrible sufferings that have just been inflicted on my people, and of which the chiefs who accompany me here have been the horrified witnesses.

It is my duty to inform the Governments assembled in Geneva, responsible as they are for the lives of millions of men, women and children, of the deadly peril which threatens them, by describing to them the fate which has been suffered by Ethiopia.

It is not only upon warriors that the Italian government has made war. It has above all attacked populations far removed from hostilities, in order to terrorize and exterminate them.

At the beginning, towards the end of 1935, Italian aircraft hurled upon my armies bombs of tear-gas. Their effects were but slight. The soldiers learned to scatter, waiting until the wind had rapidly dispersed the poisonous gases. The Italian aircraft then resorted to mustard gas. Barrels of liquid were hurled upon armed groups. But this means also was not effective; the liquid affected only a few soldiers, and barrels upon the ground were themselves a warning to troops and to the population of the danger.

It was at the time when the operations for the encircling of Makalle were taking place that the Italian command, fearing a rout, followed the procedure which it is now my duty to denounce to the world. Special sprayers were installed on board aircraft so that they could vaporize, over vast areas of territory, a fine, death-dealing rain. Groups of nine, fifteen, eighteen aircraft followed one another so that the fog issuing from them formed a continuous sheet. It was thus that, as from the end of January, 1936, soldiers, women, children, cattle, rivers, lakes and pastures were drenched continually with this deadly rain. In order to kill off systematically all living creatures, in order to more surely poison waters and pastures, the Italian command made its aircraft pass over and over again. That was its chief method of warfare.

Ravage and Terror

The refinement of this barbarism consisted in carrying ravage and terror into the most densely populated parts of the territory, the points farthest removed from the scene of hostilities. The object was to scatter fear and death over a great part of the Ethiopian territory.

These fearful tactics succeeded. Men and animals succumbed. The deadly rain that fell from the aircraft made all those whom it touched fly shrieking with pain. All those who drank the poisoned water or ate the infected food also succumbed in dreadful suffering. In tens of thousands, the victims of the Italian mustard gas fell. It is in order to denounce to the civilized world the tortures inflicted upon the Ethiopian people that I resolved to come to Geneva. None other than myself and my brave companions in arms could bring the League of Nations the undeniable proof. The appeals of my delegates addressed to the League of Nations had remained without any answer; my delegates had not been witnesses. That is why I decided to come myself to bear witness against the crime perpetrated against my people and give Europe a warning of the doom that awaits it, if it should bow before the accomplished fact.

Is it necessary to remind the Assembly of the various stages of the Ethiopian drama? For 20 years past, either as Heir Apparent, Regent of the Empire, or as Emperor, I have never ceased to use all my efforts to bring my country the benefits of civilization, and in particular to establish relations of good neighbourliness with adjacent powers. In particular I succeeded in concluding with Italy the Treaty of

Friendship of 1928, which absolutely prohibited the resort, under any pretext whatsoever, to force of arms, substituting for force and pressure the conciliation and arbitration on which civilized nations have based international order.

Country More United

In its report of October 5th 1935, the Committee of Thirteen recognized my effort and the results that I had achieved. The Governments thought that the entry of Ethiopia into the League, whilst giving that country a new guarantee for the maintenance of her territorial integrity and independence, would help her to reach a higher level of civilization. It does not seem that in Ethiopia today there is more disorder and insecurity than in 1923. On the contrary, the country is more united and the central power is better obeyed.

I should have procured still greater results for my people if obstacles of every kind had not been put in the way by the Italian Government, the Government which stirred up revolt and armed the rebels. Indeed the Rome Government, as it has today openly proclaimed, has never ceased to prepare for the conquest of Ethiopia. The Treaties of Friendship it signed with me were not sincere; their only object was to hide its real intention from me. The Italian Government asserts that for 14 years it has been preparing for its present conquest. It therefore recognizes today that when it supported the admission of Ethiopia to the League of Nations in 1923, when it concluded the Treaty of Friendship in 1928, when it signed the Pact of Paris outlawing war, it was deceiving the whole world.

The Ethiopian Government was, in these solemn treaties, given additional guarantees of security which would enable it to achieve further progress along the specific path of reform on which it had set its feet, and to which it was devoting all its strength and all its heart.

Wal-Wal Pretext

The Wal-Wal incident, in December, 1934, came as a thunderbolt to me. The Italian provocation was obvious and I did not hesitate to appeal to the League of Nations. I invoked the provisions of the treaty of 1928, the principles of the Covenant; I urged the procedure of conciliation and arbitration.

Unhappily for Ethiopia this was the time when a certain Government considered that the European situation made it imperative at all costs to obtain the friendship of Italy. The price paid was the abandonment of Ethiopian independence to the greed of the Italian Government. This secret agreement, contrary to the obligations of the Covenant, has exerted a great influence over the course of events. Ethiopia and the whole world have suffered and are still suffering today its disastrous consequences.

This first violation of the Covenant was followed by many others. Feeling itself encouraged in its policy against Ethiopia, the Rome Government feverishly made war preparations, thinking that the concerted pressure which was beginning to be exerted on the Ethiopian Government, might perhaps overcome the resistance of my people to Italian domination.

The time had to come; thus all sorts of difficulties were placed in the way with a view to breaking up the procedure; of conciliation and arbitration. All kinds of obstacles were placed in the way of that procedure. Governments tried to prevent the Ethiopian Government from finding arbitrators amongst their nationals: when once the arbitral tribunal was set up pressure was exercised so that an award favourable to Italy should be given.

All this was in vain: the arbitrators, two of whom were Italian officials, were forced to recognize unanimously that in the Wal-Wal incident, as in the subsequent incidents, no international responsibility was to be attributed to Ethiopia.

Peace Efforts

Following on this award the Ethiopian Government sincerely thought that an era of friendly relations might be opened with Italy. I loyally offered my hand to the Roman Government.

The Assembly was informed by the report of the Committee of Thirteen, dated October 5th, 1935, of the details of the events which occurred after the month of December, 1934, and up to October 3rd, 1935.

It will be sufficient if I quote a few of the conclusions of that report Nos. 24, 25 and 26 "The Italian memorandum (containing the complaints made by Italy) was laid on the Council table on September 4th, 1935, whereas Ethiopia's first appeal to the Council had been made on December 14th, 1934. In the interval between these two dates, the Italian Government opposed the consideration of the question by the Council on the ground that the only appropriate procedure was that provided for in the Italo-Ethiopian Treaty of 1928. Throughout the whole of that period, moreover, the despatch of Italian troops to East Africa was proceeding. These shipments of troops were represented to the Council by the Italian Government as necessary for the defense of its colonies menaced by Ethiopia's preparations. Ethiopia, on the contrary, drew attention to the official pronouncements made in Italy which, in its opinion, left no doubt "as to the hostile intentions of the Italian Government."

From the outset of the dispute, the Ethiopian Government has sought a settlement by peaceful means. It has appealed to the procedures of the Covenant. The Italian Government desiring to keep strictly to the procedures of the Italo-Ethiopian Treaty of 1928, the Ethiopian Government assented. It invariably stated that it would faithfully carry out the arbitral award even if the decision went against it. It agreed that the question of the ownership of Wal-Wal should not be dealt with by the arbitrators, because the Italian Government would not agree to such a course. It asked the Council to despatch neutral observers and offered to lend itself to any enquiries upon which the Council might decide.

Once the Wal-Wal dispute had been settled by arbitration, however, the Italian Government submitted its detailed memorandum to the Council in support of its claim to liberty of action. It asserted that a case like that of Ethiopia cannot be settled by the means provided by the Covenant.

It stated that, "since this question affects vital interest and is of primary importance to Italian security and civilization" it "would be failing in its most elementary duty, did it not cease once and for all to place any confidence in Ethiopia, reserving full liberty to adopt any measures that may become necessary to ensure the safety of its colonies and to safeguard its own interests."

Covenant Violated

Those are the terms of the report of the Committee of Thirteen. The Council and the Assembly unanimously adopted the conclusion that the Italian Government had violated the Covenant and was in a state of aggression. I did not hesitate to declare that I did not wish for war, that it was imposed upon me, and I should struggle solely for the independence and integrity of my people, and that in that struggle I was the defender of the cause of all small States exposed to the greed of a powerful neighbour.

In October 1935, the 52 nations who are listening to me today gave me an assurance that the aggressor would not triumph, that the resources of the Covenant would be employed in order to ensure the reign of right and the failure of violence.

I ask the fifty-two nations not to forget today the policy upon which they embarked eight months ago, and on faith of which I directed the resistance of my people against the aggressor whom they had denounced to the world.

Despite the inferiority of my weapons, the complete lack of aircraft, artillery, munitions, hospital services, my confidence in the League was absolute. I thought it to be impossible that fifty-two nations, including the most powerful in the world, should be successfully opposed by a single aggressor. Counting on the faith due to treaties, I had made no preparation for war, and that is the case with certain small countries in Europe.

When the danger became more urgent, being aware of my responsibilities towards my people, during the first six months of 1935 I tried to acquire armaments. Many Governments proclaimed an embargo to prevent my doing so, whereas the Italian Government through the Suez Canal, was given all facilities for transporting without cessation and without protest, troops, arms, and munitions.

Forced to Mobilize

On October 3rd, 1935, the Italian troops invaded my territory. A few hours later, I decreed general mobilization. In my desire to maintain peace I had, following the example of a great country in Europe on the eve of the Great War, caused my troops to withdraw thirty kilometres so as to remove any pretext of provocation.

War then took place in the atrocious conditions which I have laid before the Assembly. In that unequal struggle between a Government commanding more than forty-two million inhabitants, having at its disposal financial, industrial and technical means which enabled it to create unlimited quantities of the most death-dealing weapons, and, on the other side, a small people of twelve million inhabitants, without arms, without resources, having on its side only the justice of its own cause and the promise of the League of Nations. What real assistance was given to Ethiopia by the fifty two nations who had declared the Rome Government guilty of a breach of the Covenant and had undertaken to prevent the triumph of the aggressor?

Has each of the States' Members, as it was its duty to do by virtue of its signature appended to Article 15 of the Covenant, considered the aggressor as having committed an act of war personally directed against itself? I had placed all my hopes in the execution of these undertakings. My confidence had been confirmed by the repeated declarations made in the Council to the effect that aggression must not be rewarded, and that force would end by being compelled to bow before right.

In December, 1935, the Council made it quite clear that its feelings were in harmony with those of hundreds of millions of people who, in all parts of the world, had protested against the proposal to dismember Ethiopia. It was constantly repeated that there was not merely a conflict between the Italian Government and the League of Nations, and that is why I personally refused all proposals to my personal advantage made to me by the Italian Government, if only I would betray my people and the Covenant of the League of Nations.

I was defending the cause of all small peoples who are threatened with aggression.

What of Promises?

What has become of the promises made to me as long ago as October, 1935? I noted with grief, but without surprise that three Powers considered their undertakings under the Covenant as absolutely of no value. Their connections with Italy impelled them to refuse to take any measures whatsoever in order to stop Italian aggression. On the contrary, it was a profound disappointment to me to learn the attitude of a certain Government which, whilst ever protesting its scrupulous attachment to the Covenant, has tirelessly used all its efforts to prevent its observance. As soon as any measure which was likely to be rapidly effective was proposed, various pretexts were devised in order to postpone even consideration of the measure. Did the secret agreements of January, 1935, provide for this tireless obstruction?

The Ethiopian Government never expected other Governments to shed their soldiers' blood to defend the Covenant when their own immediately personal interests were not at stake. Ethiopian warriors asked only for means to defend themselves. On many occasions I have asked for financial assistance for the purchase of arms That assistance has been constantly refused me. What, then, in practice, is the meaning of Article 16 of the Covenant and of collective security?

The Ethiopian Government's use of the railway from Djibouti to Addis Ababa was in practice hazardous as regards transport of arms intended for the Ethiopian forces. At the present moment this is the chief, if not the only means of supply for the Italian armies of occupation.

The rules of neutrality should have prohibited transports intended for Italian forces, but there is not even neutrality since Article 16 lays upon every State Member of the League the duty not to remain a neutral but to come to the aid not of the aggressor but of the victim of aggression. Has the Covenant been respected? Is it today being respected?

Finally a statement has just been made in their Parliaments by the Governments of certain Powers, amongst them the most influential members of the League of Nations, that since the aggressor has succeeded in occupying a large part of Ethiopian territory, they propose not to continue the application of any economic and financial measures that may have been decided upon against the Italian Government.

These are the circumstances in which at the request of the Argentine Government, the Assembly of the League of Nations meets to consider the situation created by Italian aggression.

I assert that the problem submitted to the Assembly today is a much wider one. It is not merely a question of the settlement of Italian aggression.

League Threatened

It is collective security: it is the very existence of the League of Nations. It is the confidence that each State is to place in international treaties. It is the value of promises made to small States that their integrity and their independence shall be respected and ensured. It is the principle of the equality of States on the one hand, or otherwise the obligation laid upon smail Powers to accept the bonds of vassalship. In a word, it is international morality that is at stake. Have the signatures appended to a Treaty value only in so far as the signatory Powers have a personal, direct and immediate interest involved?

No subtlety can change the problem or shift the grounds of the discussion. It is in all sincerity that I submit these considerations to the Assembly. At a time when my people are threatened with extermination, when the support of the League may ward off the final blow, may I be allowed to speak with complete frankness, without reticence, in all directness such as is demanded by the rule of equality as between all States Members of the League?

Apart from the Kingdom of the Lord there is not on this earth any nation that is superior to any other. Should it happen that a strong Government finds it may with impunity destroy a weak people, then the hour strikes for that weak people to appeal to the League of Nations to give its judgment in all freedom. God and history will remember your judgment.

Assistance Refused

I have heard it asserted that the inadequate sanctions already applied have not achieved their object. At no time, and under no circumstances could sanctions that were intentionally inadequate, intentionally badly applied, stop an aggressor. This is not a case of the impossibility of stopping an aggressor but of the refusal to stop an aggressor. When Ethiopia requested and requests that she should be given financial assistance, was that a measure which it was impossible to apply whereas financial assistance of the League has been granted, even in times of peace, to two countries and exactly to the two countries who have refused to apply sanctions against the aggressor?

Faced by numerous violations by the Italian Government of all international treaties that prohibit resort to arms, and the use of barbarous methods of warfare, it is my painful duty to note that the initiative has today been taken with a view to raising sanctions. Does this initiative not mean in practice the abandonment of Ethiopia to the aggressor? On the very eve of the day when I was about to attempt a supreme effort in the defense of my people before this Assembly does not this initiative deprive Ethiopia of one of her last chances to succeed in obtaining the support and guarantee of States Members? Is that the guidance the League of Nations and each of the States Members are entitled to expect from the great Powers when they assert their right and their duty to guide the action of the League?

Placed by the aggressor face to face with the accomplished fact, are States going to set up the terrible precendent of bowing before force?

Your Assembly will doubtless have laid before it proposals for the reform of the Covenant and for rendering more effective the guarantee of collective security. Is it the Covenant that needs reform? What undertakings can have any value if the will to keep them is lacking? It is international morality which is at stake and not the Articles of the Covenant.

On behalf of the Ethiopian people, a member of the League of Nations, I request the Assembly to take all measures proper to ensure respect for the Covenant. I renew my protest against the violations of treaties of which the Ethiopian people have been the victim. I declare in the face of the whole world that the Emperor, the Government and the people of Ethiopia will not bow before force; that they maintain their claims that they will use all means in their power to ensure the triumph of right and the respect of the Covenant.

I ask the fifty-two nations, who have given the Ethiopian people a promise to help them in their resistance to the aggressor, what are they willing to do for Ethiopia? And the great Powers who have promised the guarantee of collective security to small States on whom weighs the threat that they may one day suffer the fate of Ethiopia, I ask what measures do you intend to take?

Representatives of the World, I have come to Geneva to discharge in your midst the most painful of the duties of the head of a State. What reply shall I have to take back to my people?

June, 1936

Appendix II

Address on Racial Discrimination

by Emperor Haile Selassie

The spectre of racial discrimination which has for so long cast its dark and evil shadow over much of this globe is slowly disappearing.

Men are coming increasingly to be judged by their talents and abilities rather than by the less meaningful and far more superficial standards of race and religion. But there yet remain those who, in their bigotry and ignorance, resist this flooding tide, and it is against these that our efforts must be directed. The struggle to win for our brothers in South Africa that status as free men, free to stand, heads high, among free men as equals, which so many millions of Africans and Asians have attained but yesterday, goes on. our duty is not discharged, our course is not run, our victory not won so long as apartheid, the legitimized policy of the Government of the Union of South Africa, prevails in any area of the world.

In South Africa, an attempt has been made to legislate the inequality of the races. This attempt is doomed to failure. We here are all pledged not to pause in this strife until its emptiness and mockery are revealed for all to see and those who have used it for their own purposes have abjured this doctrine which is an insult to all men and to Almighty God in Whose image we are created. But, at the same time, let us not bemuse ourselves with the notion that it is any more possible to legislate equality, for these matters concern attitudes and values over which intellect sadly exercises but little control. Let us not recoil in hatred against those who, even while protecting their freedom from bias and prejudice, reveal by their actions that the poison of discrimination has left its lasting effects, and by this reaction reveal that we, no less than they, are prey to unreasoning emotion, that we, no less than they, are susceptible to that virus which is called intolerance.

Apartheid Must Be Discredited

The African states have already imposed direct sanctions in the economic and diplomatic fields in an attempt to influence the policies of South Africa and to convince the South African leaders that it is in no sense in their interest any longer to adhere to this policy. We should, during this Confcrence, consider if there are not additional measures which we may adopt to speed the inevitable day when the policy of racial discrimination and the principle of apartheid are discredited and abandoned.

But let us take pride in the fact that as free men we attack and abhor racial discrimination on principle, wherever it is found and in whatever guise. We can, in addition to the economic pressures of which we dispose, bring our moral weight to bear and rally world opinion to our cause by revealing the brutality, the inhumanity, the inherent viciousness and evil represented by this policy.

It is only natural for man to strive towards a better life, to wish to educate his children while he himself was uneducated, to desire to shelter and clothe them while he himself was naked and scourged by the elements, to strive to spare them from the crude diseases by which he himself was ravaged. But when these ends are realized at the expense of others, at the cost of their degradation and poverty, these desires, which are not intrinsically immoral or pernicious in themselves, must be frustrated, and the means by which these otherwise legitimate ends are sought to be attained must be scorned and shunned.

We ourselves, the Non-Aligned Nations of the world, seek no less than others these same objectives. And it is not by mere chance that we also count among our number the great majority of the underdeveloped nations of the world, for not until the direction and determination of man's fate is firmly within his own grasp can he devote the totality of his strength to his own good.

SOME PERSONAL OBSERVATIONS

I am an optimist by nature—about my native land, about my family, about the world in general. I think that a positive, confident outlook can be the precursor of good things t o come. I once heard a story that illustrates this kind of thinking, albeit in reverse fashion.

A man was working on a railroad refrigerator car located on a rail siding. He was experienced in his work and was really an expert in railroad refrigeration systems. While he was busy doing his job a switch engine accidentally bumped the train o f which his car was a part. The car door clanked shut and automatically locked itself. He could not open it from the inside. He was aware that a person could survive only about six hours in the refrigerated climate of his car. So his first reaction was to start pounding on the door and screaming and yelling for help. No one heard, and after about an hour he gave up.

For the next two hours he pondered his fate, and after finding a sharp tool with which he could scrape his final thoughts on the car floor, he said to his family and friends. "I am beginning to get numb. The chill has gone through my bones and I am finding it difficult to think. I expect to die in about two hours." Finally, with only half an hour left, he wrote: "I won't be able to write much longer because my mind has gone dim. I feel the breath of death coming over me." At which point he fell over dead.

When the car was opened later that day, they found him still gripping his writing tool in a hand already stiffened by death. But they also found, to their amazement, that the refrigeration unit had not been turned on! He just thought it was, and met his demise by assuming that he would die. So die he did.

When living for a time in England, I discovered some very interesting groups whose common aims were to study and discuss individual values, individuals i n society, individual self-awareness and individuals in their environments. What I brought away from these meetings was an appreciation of the extent to which our lives are influenced by the environment in which each of us lives, and the need for answers t o such questions as: Who am I? Why am I here? Where I am going? Why do so many of us hate each other? The answers can be found only through self-searching—an exercise that should be individually fulfilling and collectively healthy.

May you have your full share of happy days.